HIDDEN TREASURES

Find Yours!

HIDDEN TREASURES : Find Yours!

ISBN-10: 0-9988869-0-4
ISBN-13: 978-0-9988869-0-9

Printed in the United States of America

A special big thanks to Julie Pendray for doing some of the editing in this book.

Hidden Treasures

Find Yours!

Bowman Publishing
U.S.A.

Dedication
by
Pastor Jesús Sandoval

———◇═══◇═══◇———

To my beautiful wife Stephanie, (a.k.a.) red fox, my four lovely children: Ruben (a.k.a.) Munchy; Annabelle my princess; Andrew my mini me; and Maya my cuddle bug.

To my parents, Jesús and Herlinda Sandoval and my grandmother "mama concha." Rest in peace.

To the loudest family you will ever meet—the Sandovals—my only sister Lucia, my oldest brother Gabriel, and my other brothers, Luis (a.k.a.) Gordo and Manuel, the youngest.

To all of my aunts, uncles and cousins. The list is way too long to mention all of them by name, but you know you're close to my heart.

To all of my friends that have already entered eternity. I love you and I miss you very much.

To all of those that are behind bars; you're not forgotten!

To our pastors Clem and Maria Casas, our leadership pastors Richard and Nancy Salazar, and all of New Harvest Christian Fellowship.

To my New Harvest Church family of East San Diego, to whom I have committed my life to serve and love.

To those who serve alongside, shoulder to shoulder, the core! The list is really long.

To my Tijuana Bible study family.

To my Heavenly Father, Jesus my Savior, and the Holy Spirit my comforter and guide.

Collaborators for Community Mentoring and Healing

Community Partnerships & Collaborations

County of San Diego Health & Human Services Agency
County of San Diego Probation Department
San Diego City Council
San Diego Mayor's Office
San Diego Police Department

Schools

Alliant International University
Central Elementary
Cherokee Point Elementary
Garfield Hoover High
Horace Mann Middle
San Diego State University
Wilson Middle

Churches

Calvary Lutheran
New Harvest Christian Fellowship
Sure Harvest

Grassroots

Community Assistance Support Team (C.A.S.T.)
Community Mentors
Community Wraparound
Mothers with a Message
Orphan Frontier
Project AWARE
San Diego Compassion Project (SDCP)
Youth Empowerment
Youth Voice

Community Based Organizations

Community Connections For Youth (CCFY)
Fred Finch Youth Center
Harmonium, Inc.
Jackie Robinson YMCA of Southeast
Metro United Urban Ministries
Mi Casa Corp.
National Conflict Resolution Center (NCRC)
Oasis Clubhouse
Price-Copley YMCA of City Heights
Union of Pan Asian Communities (UPAC)
Urban League of San Diego County

Dedication

by

Arthur Soriano

To my beautiful wife, Gabby Soriano, and all my kids. To our mothers, Aleyda Wales and Modesta Hernandez. A mother's love is like no other. A mother's prayer is like no other. Your prayers broke our chains. For all of you in juvenile hall, prisons and systems, and for families connected: It can be done.

Thank you Pastor Jesús Sandoval for inspiring me

Forward

by
Dana Brown
City of San Diego Commission
on Gang Prevention & Intervention

———————◇══◇═◇═◇══◇———————

Hidden Treasures is a message of hope and healing, including many individuals sharing their hearts about the trauma and pain they've endured in their lives. They also share their journeys of transformation. You'll be uplifted and inspired with the bravery written through their own words reflecting horrific challenges and heartbreaking experiences. You'll be greatly moved to read the progressions in their lives that gave them the courage to make positive changes in their own lives, so much that they now influence organizations and systems to focus on helping the people they serve to heal.

Many of us featured in this book have known each other for years. Now, the interweaving of the individuals expressing their hearts has developed into grass roots organizations collaborating with faith based organizations, community based organizations, schools, and top city and county agencies. Truly it has become grass roots to grass tops, influencing everyone in understanding about the impact of trauma on our brain and body just as we understand our capacity to heal and build on our resilience.

You will read the narratives of youths, parents, siblings, community leaders and systems leaders as you navigate through *Hidden Treasures*. You will learn from many traumatized individuals who will inspire your own healing journey. You will be ignited to impact healing change in your own neighborhood and community.

Hidden Treasures is a road map of discovering your own Hidden Treasure.

We have presented a list within this book of all these organizations, grass roots and community based, churches, schools and systems who are collaborative partners, in case you want to reach out for additional information on their role with bringing healing to our communities.

Comments

by
Jason M. Rasch
Supervising Probation Officer
San Diego County Probation Department
Special Operations Division, Juvenile Gang Intervention
and Intensive Supervision Unit

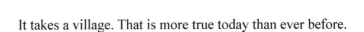

It takes a village. That is more true today than ever before.

As a community, we must work together in providing opportunities for our youth. Collaboration between law enforcement, schools, faith based practitioners, mental health and community mentors is an integral part in the development, support, and success of every youth. Mentoring through active listening, sharing, and having genuine compassion is the recipe for growth and significant change, in attitude, belief, and perception. Since the inception of the relationship between the Probation Department and those committed to Community Wraparound, we have witnessed success in changing the lives of youth, mentors, law enforcement, and community partners in a positive way.

It is relationships such as these that pave the way for new alternatives in working with youth and its progressive spirit motivates all those involved to push forward for the betterment of our community.

Comments

by
Prof. Lynn Sharpe-Underwood
Alliant International University

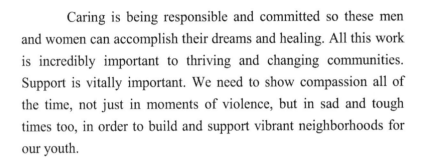

Caring is being responsible and committed so these men and women can accomplish their dreams and healing. All this work is incredibly important to thriving and changing communities. Support is vitally important. We need to show compassion all of the time, not just in moments of violence, but in sad and tough times too, in order to build and support vibrant neighborhoods for our youth.

To date in partnership with Alliant International University/Professional Community Training Institute, we have served fifty community mentors/student partners. Pastor Sandoval and Arthur Soriano are learning facilitators of this effort. They bring local knowledge and important viewpoints to the effort.

The mission of the Community Collaborative of Community Mentors is to facilitate and provide support of community practitioners who wish to enhance their knowledge and strengthen their professional education using public health and public safety frameworks.

Other partners in this effort include San Diego County Health and Human Services, the Probation Department, San Diego City Police, Alliance for Community Empowerment, National

Conflict Resolution Center, Fred Finch Youth Center, and the California Endowment.

Contents

Introduction
by
Pastor Jesús Sandoval
Founder of Hidden Treasures

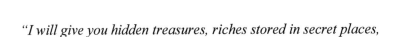

"I will give you hidden treasures, riches stored in secret places,
so that you may know that I am the LORD..."
— Isaiah 45:3

This is a true story. My parents sold a vacant lot in Uruapan, Michoacán in Mexico. The people who purchased the land began constructing a hall now known as El Salon Crystal. As they began to lay the foundation and dig through the surface of the land, they discovered a hidden treasure, pots filled with gold centenarios.

The entire time, in what seemed to be a worthless lot, my parents had a hidden treasure underneath all the dirt.

I began to wonder how many people have a hidden treasure in their own lives underneath all the dirt of life, underneath all the pain and trauma. Beneath the surface I believe you have a hidden treasure!

This book *Hidden Treasures,* is a collection of community testimonials of people who went from trauma to triumph. These folks know each other and work closely together in the community of San Diego City Heights, Central and South Eastern regions.

We are hoping that these stories can inspire those who are on the journey of finding their purpose or "hidden treasure." We believe everyone has their own story of triumph and if you keep searching and digging you will find yours.

We hope this book will be the beginning of a series. I want to acknowledge all those who contributed to this first *Hidden Treasures* book. Without you, this would not have been possible. To those who didn't make it into this book, you will be able to participate in another one of the series.

It is my hope to share all the hidden treasures, the untold stories of trauma to triumph, that have been buried in our community of San Diego with the rest of California, the United States, and all around the world.

Peace and Blessings,

Pastor Jesús Sandoval

A Word
by
Arthur Soriano

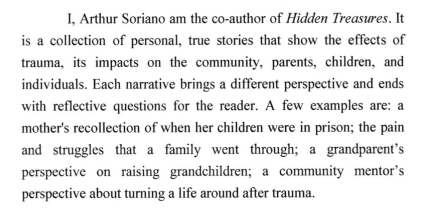

I, Arthur Soriano am the co-author of *Hidden Treasures*. It is a collection of personal, true stories that show the effects of trauma, its impacts on the community, parents, children, and individuals. Each narrative brings a different perspective and ends with reflective questions for the reader. A few examples are: a mother's recollection of when her children were in prison; the pain and struggles that a family went through; a grandparent's perspective on raising grandchildren; a community mentor's perspective about turning a life around after trauma.

These powerful narratives provide hope and support.

Chapter 1
Hidden Memories

Pastor Jesús Sandoval

Who said Children Don't Remember? Everything has a beginning. I can remember my mom holding me in her arms as I was drinking a baby bottle of water and she was talking to my Tia in the kitchen. I was wearing nothing but a diaper. It was about noontime and it was a very hot day. I was about one year old.

During this season of my life, we lived in Boca Raton, Florida where my parents worked in a camp where they farmed tomatoes. My dad and my uncle were in charge of dropping all the workers off at the fields each day, and my mom and my Tia stayed back to cook the meals for all of them. Sometime around 1978 my family had migrated from Uruapan, Michoacán, which is about a four-hour drive south of Guadalajara, Mexico.

My sister Lucia, who is about four years older than I am, spent her days playing in the fields throwing tomatoes and playing with one of our only friends "Chile" who was the most playful dog, a brownish, silky smooth Doberman.

El Cuba is another flash in my mind. One early afternoon two vans pulled up. They were white with a green stripe in the middle. I recall hearing one of my adult amigos, who everyone called el Cuba because he was Cuban, running towards me. He was in the same isle I was playing in. He began yelling "la migra! la migra!!" He picked me up and threw me over his shoulder and galloped across the field into the thick brush where everyone else had gone. I remember all of us waiting to see if they would come after us, but after a few minutes the vans drove off. Thank God for el Cuba. That could have been the last time I saw my family. After that happened, I had to stay back in the kitchen with my mom and Tia and my sister. I remember in those days there was another worker everyone called el Huevon, which means lazy, because he wouldn't work in the fields. Somehow he became the security. He was another set of eyes for my dad and uncles in a group of about 80 to 100 workers.

Reader Reflection

My earliest childhood memory is:

_____

_____

_____

_____

_____

_____

_____

_____

_____

CHAPTER 1

A lighter shade of poverty

By the time I was three years old, all the workers on the ranch had grown to love me because I was the only kid besides my sister. I remember every time they got paid I would grab a paper bag from the kitchen and go collect at least a dollar from each worker. I would come back with my pockets full of dollar bills. I got my little hustle started early. I would also take cold beers from the kitchen and take them back to the workers.

Michael Jackson's song "Beat It" was my favorite at the time. I remember watching his music videos and mimicking his dance moves. I remember a bus picking me up when I turned four and started pre-school. Later, I found out that I was the only boy being picked up in front of the field, about one-hundred yards from where we lived. In comparison to all the other kids with two-story homes, mine looked like a little brick room, which it was. I still remember the day the teacher asked all the students to draw what their homes looked like. Everyone drew big houses with swimming pools in their back yards. I felt so embarrassed to draw my home that I copied my best friend Mark's house. He was sitting next to me. When it came time for everyone to share their pictures, about half the kids knew that it wasn't my house which I drew because these kids were the same ones who rode on the bus. It wasn't long before I realized I was different.

We now know that poverty is connected to elevated chronic stress, which can increase the vulnerability of a child's development. Back then, all I knew was that everyone else's parents would come and visit the class to volunteer and sit in. My parents could not come because of transportation. The school was predominantly white upper middle class.

Mark was my best friend. He and his mom used to pick me up and bring me to their beautiful two-story home. I remember walking into his home. I had never seen the inside of his house before. He also had his own playroom with all the toys a boy could ever want. I was in another world. After a couple of hours of playing indoors, we went outside to ride bikes. He had a new bike, so he let me borrow his first bike. He took off, only to find out I still didn't know how to ride a bike. I felt so embarrassed. He turned around and came back and told me, "You're gonna have to learn on my little sister's bike." It still had training wheels on it. Mark never made fun of me but always looked out for me. It seemed as if he knew he was exposing me to new experiences. I eventually learned to ride on a bike my pops bought for me at a yard sale. I still remember it was a small blue Schwinn with a banana seat and big handle bars.

One of my last memories of Florida was when I came home after school and in my parents' room they had one of those small fridges with a TV on top of it. I served myself some rice krispies and turned the TV on to watch cartoons. That day, pops was home and was taking a nap. All of a sudden my mom walked in with another lady I had never seen. My mom jumped on the bed and slapped my dad on his chest. Dad woke up in shock and pinned my mom underneath him. My mom began to yell at dad and the lady. Apparently, they had something going on. I saw a different side of moms that day. My dad got up and took off in his truck and my mom stayed back crying on the bed. I looked up at the lady, then she walked out. I tried everything I could to comfort my mom. By the time my sister got home a couple of hours had passed by, my mom was on the phone making arrangements with my grandmother (my dad's mom) to fly back to San Diego. I had a piggy bank that I broke that evening to give moms all the money I was saving to help her with the cost. We didn't leave immediately. It took a few months, maybe a year, because in the process my mom and dad had made up and my younger brother Luis was born.

By the time we came back to San Diego it was around 1983. My older brother, Gabriel, had stayed back with my grandmother and was raised in East San Diego, now known as City Heights or Mid-City.

I remember watching Gabriel getting dressed for school every morning and taking extra time to iron his clothes. He used to put creases on his white T-shirts and crease up his dickies as he listened to oldies in the morning, or one of the local radio stations.

Gabriel attended Wilson Middle School and I was placed in Central Elementary School. I was first placed in Ms. Cisneros' class until they found out I couldn't read Spanish. Then I was transferred to Ms. Trudo's class until they found out I couldn't read English. I felt out of place and completely embarrassed. Thank God for the patience of Mrs. Johnson who taught me how to read using flash cards. She would pull me out for about an hour each day throughout the next couple of years.

"Criss cross, apple sauce." We were transitioning into a reading circle, where we sat Indian style, when all of a sudden Roberto, who was sitting next to me, shouted in a loud voice and everyone could hear, "Jesús is wearing girls' shoes."

I stood up, quickly realizing I'd forgotten to fill in the baby blue dots at the bottom of a pair of girls' Reebok shoes my mom had bought me at a yard sale. For the most part, I had covered the noticeable girly outline with a black marker, except for the bottom of the shoes. I rebutted and said, "No, I'm not." I knew they'd started to stare at my shoes. They all realized that I had traced the baby blue outline of my shoes with a black marker. I was about 8 years old and in the third grade. I remember the blood rushing to my head and that funny feeling you feel in your stomach when you feel humiliated. Poverty was the norm for many of us growing up "trying to make a dollar out of fifteen cents."

Reader Reflection

Do you remember growing up poor? How did you feel? How did you deal with it? What memories or effects do you think you might still have from it today? Explain:

_____

_____

_____

_____

_____

_____

_____

_____

_____

_____

_____

_____

_____

_____

_____

_____

My Jefitos Sacrifice *(My Parents' Sacrifice)*

My parents were always loving and caring and provided all they could. Yet, the rent and bills in San Diego kept increasing. My pops worked fixing cars by day and worked at Café Coyote's many other Mexican restaurants singing in the Old Town area of San Diego. He is still there after all these years, so if you stop by, make sure you drop a fat tip. Moms worked at a convalescent home doing the laundry and cleaning. When she got home she wouldn't stop. Mom makes the best frijoles (beans). We would always comment about her making beans and selling them. We still joke about it today.

I remember my father telling me all the things he went through as a child, being the oldest of four at the age of twelve when my grandfather, a taxi driver, died. My dad was left with my grandmother to help raise his three younger siblings. He did all he could to put food on the table. He sacrificed his childhood for his family and so did moms. He never really had a male figure to learn how to be a husband and father.

Because of my parents' work ethic and disconnection from the outside neighborhood, my older brother's friends, who had each other's backs, formed a bond and later joined a gang.

Reader Reflection

What sacrifices have you or your family made? How has that effected you?

_____

_____

_____

_____

_____

_____

_____

_____

_____

_____

Gazing at the stars in the sky!

By the time I was sixteen years old, I had been stabbed and shot. It happened in the alley of the Jack in the Box on El Cajon Boulevard and Euclid with a shotgun. Thank God for Morro who distracted the shooter from shooting me a second time. He took a bullet for me. Then "lil Mike" came around the corner, speeding in his Cadillac, and rushed me to the hospital. As he sped along El Cajon Boulevard, doing about 50 mph, the cops began chasing us thinking we had shot someone. He wouldn't stop. He was determined to get me to Mercy Hospital. Morro and I sat wounded and gasping for air. Lil Mike continued driving. By that time, the helicopter, known as the ghetto bird, was on us with the light. Lil Mike ended up stopping on 40th Street because of all the traffic and he didn't want to crash! There must have been at least 10 cop cars and officers with guns drawn instructing us to get out one at a time with hands up. The only problem was I couldn't lift my left arm. I couldn't even feel it. It was numb. Then Mikey yelled out, "He's shot. He can't move!" The officers laid me on the ground and the paramedics took me and Morro to the hospital.

You would have thought this was going to shift my reckless behavior but it only propelled me to continue to live life in the fast lane. I remember every year that went by losing as many as four friends, not including those who got locked up for a very long time. Some are still in prison today. I thought I was not going to make it to my 18th birthday. I remember kicking it late one night at Azalea Park, staring up at the stars and asking myself or God, what on earth was I put here for? I always knew there was more to life than the way I was living but I didn't see myself getting there. Hopelessness was my norm, even though I was good at hiding it

behind the mask.

I remember seeing a very close friend being lowered into his casket, with his children not realizing their father was in it. At that time I also had a son about two years old. I knew that could be me next time, and someone else would be raising my son. I didn't want that for him. The seed was planted, as my friend was also being planted into the earth They say God can bring life out of death and in this case He did for me.

In 1997, I met a pastor at the corner of University Avenue and 39th Street. He was a missionary who had just returned from Russia. He was handing out Christian tracts. I wanted to know more. I had burned so many bridges in the neighborhood. It was easier to open up to a stranger. This man, Clemente Casas, invited me and my girlfriend to his family home for dinner.

When I got to his home, I saw the family pictures on the wall. I felt such peace. It hit me. I wanted a family. That's really what ultimately caused me to give my life to Jesus. After dinner, the pastor led my girlfriend, Stephanie, and me in a prayer that went like this: "Lord Jesus, come into my heart. Forgive me of my sins. Teach me Your ways. Heal my heart. Guide me and direct me in the path You want to put me on."

I was the first one in our circle of friends in the neighborhood who changed. Gradually, my transformation had a domino effect. Some people were still in and out of jail. Eventually, they wore themselves out. Then they came in and hung up the gloves.

Pastor Casas was having Bible studies at home. In 1998, we moved into a storefront building, upstairs on University Avenue and Wilson Street. Our church was called New Harvest. Later, the pastor transferred his pastorship to Montebello, two hours north of San Diego. I had married Stephanie in 1998. She and I were ordained by the church fellowship in 2003. Probation officers started sending the difficult cases to me. We became known for helping felons settle back into the community and finding jobs.

Our God is a God of miracles. He radically transformed my life from 1998 onward. People often ask me, "How did you go from a life of gangs to becoming a pastor?" My answer is, "It all started with a prayer, while gazing at the stars." There is a scripture in the Bible that says, "Now to him who is able to do immeasurably more than all we ask or imagine, according to his power that is at work within us" (Ephesians 3:20). This scripture reminded me that no matter how much I tried to modify my behavior externally, it was an internal conversion that I needed.

That's where it all started. Today, nineteen years later I now have four children and a beautiful wife, and I get to see this happen every day with families in our church and community.

Our church is a spiritual hospital

My first job after my conversion was at Polinsky Children's Center, an emergency shelter for abused, abandoned and neglected children. It's strange how God would put me in a place where I would be reminded on a daily basis where my son could have ended up if I had not changed. There I found my purpose: to encourage youth who never have had opportunities. I worked there for nine years, all along building relationships with staff and residents that I still have to this day. We all need someone in our life, but not just for a season or a purpose. Someone who will stay. There is a verse in the Bible in which God promises to never leave us nor forsake us.

During that time, I faithfully served the Lord Jesus Christ with my church family in the community reaching out to all who were ready and willing. I would also see a lot of youth who had aged out of Polinsky, who needed support. Since I already had a strong rapport with them, they have stayed connected to this day. I work with some at my current job at Fred Finch Youth Center, which serves to reunify families. They work as youth partners because they have life experience. Who better to help serve than someone who has been there and done that? Isn't God amazing! This book is their story too because we were all in the same boat once upon a time. My whole life is dedicated to serving those who are hurting and healing just like I am.

Everywhere I go, I see hidden treasures all around me at my job, in my church, and all over my community, including those coming back from prison and the professionals. Even those who shot me are hidden treasures. I feel love and compassion for people. I know God put it there because I didn't have love before. Now, I have an overflow of love. That's what we all need. For God so loved the world that he gave his only begotten Son (Jesus Christ) that whosoever believes in him should not perish but have everlasting life. God doesn't want religion, he wants you. He wants a relationship with you.

In 2003, I became the senior pastor of my home church

here in San Diego. When pastors would ask me what seminary I went to, I used to get embarrassed because I barely made it out of Garfield High School. I remember when Pastor Reggie gave me a word about not feeling intimidated about that because, like David in the Bible tending his father's sheep behind the hillside, God was preparing me at Polinsky with all the families we served on a daily basis. So, now when they ask me, I say, "Polinsky seminary." God shaped me and molded me to be patient, kind, forgiving, persistent and unconditional.

I still have so much growing to do in other areas. Just ask my wife! Our church is currently made up of a mixture of ex-felons, families in the system, professionals, different cultures and backgrounds; and I wouldn't trade it for the world.

Reader Reflection:

Have you realized that good can come out of bad? Have you noticed the hidden treasure moments of your life? What are they?

_____

_____

_____

_____

_____

_____

Community Wraparound

God created us all to connect and bond, and that is what happened.

People ask why do youth join gangs? It's almost like asking why do young people have friends? Most groups like clubs and fraternities have their own culture, background and reasons why they are formed. Most groups develop a hierarchy to keep order and stability. They may organize out of a need for financial gain, safety, respect, compassion or goals within a community. There are basic, underlying needs that these groups have and this is how members identify and relate. Some are legal activities that people aspire to achieve, and others may be illegal, due to what may be accessible at the time, from generation to generation.

For example, I was once conducting a strengths assessment with a group of police officers and active gang members on probation. We were in the same room and we asked them "what qualities do police officers have?" I began to write the list on the board. "They are courageous, risk takers, team players, loyal, protectors, and they love their community. Then I asked the same question about the gang members. "They are courageous, risk takers, team players, loyal, protectors, and they love their community." The gang members realized they had the same characteristics but that each group expressed these attributes in different ways. That was a breakthrough moment! Beneath the white t-shirt and dickies and beneath the badge and uniform, they had a lot of similarities.

Our Community Wraparound program continues to reach gang-involved youth with former gang members as mentors. It's a grass roots effort. We mentors all support each other and hold each other accountable in terms of our recovery and boundaries. The group springs out of New Harvest, and so does another group, Moms With a Message. These are coordinated efforts. Other churches are also involved.

We know that in San Diego county, roughly 7,000 individuals belong to approximately 155 street gangs. The majority are in the low-income Central and South East regions. Most youth join gangs in early adolescence and 39% of gang members have at least one parent in the same gang. These young people rarely finish high school, replacing school with gang activities that include violent and non-violent crime. In fact, of the 67,621 crimes committed in San Diego in 2014, gangs were responsible for nearly 17,000 according to government agencies.

Community Wraparound promotes success through involvement with family, school, work and community. The program includes educational, civic and social components, such as individual mentoring and comprehensive life planning, family and group meetings, and community involvement and service projects. Participants are primarily low-income, gang-affiliated youth, at high risk for incarceration, criminal activity or victimization. They work with a mentoring team to design goals and strategies based on their strengths. Participants are identified and referred by San Diego Police and the County Probation Department. They target gang members who are next in line to assume leadership. The goal is to prevent them from making choices that will forever alter the course of their lives.

You can see Community Wraparound on the news. Please go to this link and watch a news clip about some good that is happening through Community Wraparound:

www.youtube.com/watch?v=STTMYGyHPW8

The success of Community Wraparound is in its collaborative, grassroots approach and the fact that it is offered both in and by the community. Key partners include: San Diego Police Department, San Diego Probation Department, New Harvest Christian Fellowship, Fred Finch Youth Center, Youth Empowerment and countless volunteers and community partners.

Chapter 2
Adverse Childhood Experiences

Arthur Soriano

I was born to Aleyda Hernandez on March 18, 1976 in the Bronx, New York. My mother was a head-turning beauty who had immigrated to the United States in 1973.

She was born in Cartago, Colombia to a family of fifteen in a poverty-stricken country where violence was normal. At age seven she started to become the leader of her siblings. That meant working and going to school at the same time, so the family could eat. My mother's way of coping was running, so she could escape her trauma. It was her self-care. Although her family was dirt-poor, they had a strong bond of love that nobody could break.

Poverty led her family to become drug traffickers for a

Colombian Cartel, running prostitution rings and being musicians for the cartel party scene. Despite the community trauma, Aleyda had morals and values that her mother Cenobia Gallegos had embedded in her. Cenobia had a strong personality. No one could get anything past her. The law in the home was firm. If you crossed her, she would beat you with a stick. The code of honor was taught in her home. If you were picked on, then you better defend yourself.

Aleyda wanted to escape the war zone mentality and be in a better place. She didn't know how but she was determined to help her mother and father break the chains of poverty. Life was extremely hard and the family did their best to survive.

At age nineteen, the thought of going to the United States to live the American Dream became a reality. Aleyda was blessed with the opportunity and flew to the Bronx. She was determined to work hard to send money home to her family. She got a job at a belt factory and worked long hours.

In the process, she met my father. He'd immigrated to New York from Ecuador before my mother. He had much more experience than she did in a country that was completely foreign to her. The culture shock was humongous to her. She was vulnerable to individuals taking advantage of her. She was an attractive young lady. That drew a lot of attention. She married my father right away. He was more than a decade older than her. She confided in him and believed that he would help her live her dream.

Then I was born. At first, their marriage was full of life. Then my trauma began. I vividly remember the domestic violence when I was a toddler. I was a scared little boy and didn't know what to do. Those memories have lived with me for a lifetime.

My mother tried her hardest to make it work. Fortunately, she began to put a plan together to get out of that unhealthy relationship. My father was a womanizer and a charmer. However, my mother grew up in an environment where she was taught the code of honor. Don't let anyone pick on you. She used the power of persuasion to influence his own friends to give him a taste of his own medicine. That's when her exit plan began.

My parents' apartment was fully furnished with brand new everything. One day, my father flew to Ecuador, as he always did. With the help of his friends, my mother cleared out the whole apartment. She sold all the furniture and was able to use the money to get her own studio. I was only four years old. My mother made a sound decision to break away from my father.

She flew me to Cartago, Colombia for a year. The stress on my brain was beginning to have an impact on my development. I went from experiencing chronic trauma to a country with a war zone mentality. I didn't know any of my family there. By this time, my grandmother "Mamita" had a big home, fully furnished with the help of my hard-working mother and the help from other family members whose lives had been lived in darkness. It was like a castle, with lots of rooms with ornaments and decorations from all around the world.

Mamita and I began to form a relationship. She loved me purely. She called me "the gringo." She embedded the code of honor in me and I respected her. The house was full of cousins, aunts and uncles. My grandfather, Ernesto Hernandez, was always out working hard. I began to create relationships with my cousins and we loved each other like siblings.

One hot sunny day I was playing futbol (soccer) with my cousins and neighborhood friends on the street in front of Mamita's house, which was a custom for us to do. We would use big rocks as the goalie poles. I was really into the soccer game but I could see a man walking on the other side of the street. Suddenly I heard the sound of a motorcycle turn the corner. It was coming at full speed. All I could see was a person with a helmet and dark clothes. The helmet-head man made a screeching stop where the man across the street was walking. I can remember clearly what transpired. The energy of the soccer game suddenly stopped. Helmet-head got of his motorcycle, walked up to the man and unloaded the clip of his gun.

Everyone scattered. It was the norm of that community. I froze. I didn't know what to do. I was in a complete state of shock. Mamita came to my rescue. By this time, the motorcycle was long gone. She yanked my ear and dragged me like a rag doll. She snapped me out of my frozen state of shock and yelled at me in Spanish, wanting to know why I had stayed there. But that norm had never been my reality. I had no choice but to learn quickly. That single traumatic event led to my acute trauma.

Everyone went about their day like it was nothing. Life in Colombia was family oriented. My cousin, Fernando, was a stone cold individual and was only a teenager at that time. He and his crew of friends lived the criminal fast lifestyle. Their behaviors stood out to me. Although I was a child I was forced to pay close attention to my environment.

On a Christmas Eve, Mamita threw a big celebration. Delicious Colombian food, empanadas and sancocho. That morning she tried to get me to snap the chicken's neck so we could eat it for dinner. I gave it a shot but I just couldn't kill the chicken. Swiftly, like a pro, she snapped the chicken's neck. Blood dripped everywhere and I had to leave the kitchen.

Everyone was happy that day. We fellowshipped, played music and ate till we couldn't eat any more. I remember Fernando coming into the home with blood stains all over his shirt, pants and shoes. He was crying. Mamita sat him down at the dinner table and gave him some agua panela (sweet water). After he calmed down a bit, he poured out his soul. His best friend, Wilson Rojas, had committed suicide. Wilson was the boyfriend of my cousin Adriana (Fernando's sister). At least that's what I was told. Fernando's pain became my pain. I was extremely sad.

My mother was getting situated in the States. I was getting spoiled with clothes and toys in the mail. But I missed my mother and wanted to be by her side. It just wasn't the same without her presence.

I was supposed to be in Colombia for a year but a turn of events sped up the process. During the eighth month, I was on Mamita's patio. She had a Doberman Pincher named Ringo. Ringo was a female who'd just had puppies. My curiosity got the best of me that day. I went to play with the puppies. Ringo suddenly attacked me. She bit my face and split the corner of my mouth half way through my cheek. She also bit my leg. The pain was excruciating. I remember screaming. Blood was everywhere. The howls could be heard throughout the room. Mamita, like always, came to my rescue with a broomstick. She began to beat the life out of Ringo. My tia (aunt) Marlene called the ambulance. I remember her hysterical screams. I ended up in the hospital for days recovering.

My mother flew all the way down to Colombia just for me and we both left as quickly as possible. I was five years old. We then stayed in New York until I was eight years old. Then my mother moved us to Anchorage, Alaska. That is where she gave her life to the Lord Jesus Christ. It was the best gift my mother could receive. He completely healed her from the traumatic events of her life.

As a kid, my mother's transformation took some getting used to. Life was good. I had a lot of energy and I began to live life as a kid should. The seeds of a Christian lifestyle were beginning to be planted. A pastor friend of my mother told her how beautiful the city of San Diego was: America's Finest City. We landed in the crime-infested melting pot of East San Diego.

Reader Reflection

Have you been able to heal from any trauma from your past?

_____

_____

_____

_____

_____

_____

Are there any unresolved issues that still haunt you?

_____

_____

_____

_____

_____

_____

_____

_____

_____

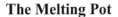

The Melting Pot

In 1988, I moved to East San Diego with my mother Aleyda. The inner-city neighborhood had the highest crime rate in San Diego County. Gang activity and drug dealing were rampant, housing was substandard and public services were lacking. It was the melting pot of the county, a rich culture, with all walks of life from everywhere. Refugees from other parts of the world came for their peace of mind. Everyone had their own story. All had their own traumas. Each individual dealt with it in their own way.

My mom and I lived in a two-bedroom home across the street from Highland Park on 44th Street. The San Diego police were there in trailers through the night to prevent crime. Immigration raids, drug dealing and gang activity were the norm.

I was barely starting to heal from the trauma I had already dealt with before. The fatherless factor played a big role in my life. I was enrolled at Wilson Middle School. I was a kid with a lot of energy, with a loss of family connection. At school, I began to make friendships that were unhealthy. I needed that sense of belonging, of being part of something. So I began to reach out to the kids who were searching for the same.

My lovely mother worked long hours cleaning houses in upscale Coronado. At times, I would go with her to keep her company. The homes were immaculately beautiful. They had all the beautiful things a family would want. Although my mom provided, we were part of "the system." Section 8 housing and food stamps were our way of life. I loved my mother's sacrifice in trying her very best. Yet, I had holes in my heart and I was trying to replace the pains with different outlets.

Being poor is related to criminal behavior. Blacks and Hispanics are more likely to be poor than Whites. Being on a low income means living in a world radically different than that of the affluent. The smarter ones in the inner city are the ones who eventually get out of their unhealthy circumstances. In 2011, 21% of White households had an income of less than $25,000 per year, while for Blacks the figure was 40% and for Hispanics the figure was 31%.

Growing up without a father can lead to juvenile delinquency and that leads to incarceration. Black kids are three times more likely to live in a single parent home than White kids (66% versus 24%). Latino kids are almost twice as likely as White kids to do so (41% versus 24%). I was a kid without a father and I had too much energy for a hard-working single mother to handle. The holes in my heart were going to get filled one way or another.

The love my mother had for me was strong but I needed more. At that time in my life, I needed male guidance. Males usually look up to other males. The East San Diego gang was in search of another generational clique. The Rascals clique was in full affect. They were allowed to run around the neighborhood like it was the thing to do. The nearest police station was miles away. Some of the main stomping grounds for the Rascals was at the Quick Corner Liquor store on 39th Street, a pool hall club, Rascal alley, a couple pizza places, and a cheap night club called La Posta.

I walked all through these areas on my way home from school. Before I knew it, I was connected. The attraction for the neighborhood became my number one priority. My gang member friends showed me love and filled my emptiness. This was now my life. In my head, it was all I wanted to live for. I loved my mother but my juvenile mentality led me to believe that this was greater than any other love.

The late 1980s and early 1990s were the prime years of gang banging. I got involved in criminal activity, thinking it was quick excitement. I didn't think of the consequences. I was all the way in and was loyal to the fullest. My friends and I were a menace to society. I stopped listening to my mother and often started running away. Many times I would be gone for weeks at a time. I would only come home to rest when I was tired of running the streets.

Crystal meth was at an all-time peak. I explored all drugs at a very young age. But crystal meth got a hold of me and the crew I ran around with. This lifestyle led me in and out of juvenile hall. At seventeen years old, after being AWOL from camp twice, I was given my last chance at Arizona Boys Ranch. It was a youth authority alternative camp run by former military staff. We had to respond "yes sir" or "no sir". It was one of the hardest things I had ever done in my life, especially the first two months because I was hard-headed and didn't go with the program. They had a place for individuals who did not go with the program. They attempted to break my criminal minded behavior. I fought against it but I saw that I would not win.

Then I decided to give that program a try. It was one of my best decisions because it taught me discipline. Also, it gave me experiences that I had never had before. For example, running a marathon, being part of a basketball team and training me to be a hot shot firefighter with the forest rangers. After I completed the program I was supposed to stay in Arizona to be a hot shot. Instead, after two weeks, I was homesick. So I went back to San Diego.

That is when my criminal mind kicked into a higher gear. I ended up right back where I started. Me and my homeboys were now older and "smarter" in our minds. In our culture at the time, guns were a part of life. Gang banging to the fullest was the way. So that's what we did. In our criminal minds, it was an illusion we were willing to die for.

I was now eighteen years old, living at the trap house (known drug house) on Chamoune Avenue, tweeking and going 100 mph. Slanging drugs and living day by day. Figuring out what the next day would bring. Our priority was the high-octane lifestyle. No one could get in our way.

On the night I lost freedom, the wind screamed. A homeboy of mine, who was an expert in stealing cars was with me that night. We were two hoodlums on an ominous mission. Our walk was silent. Something didn't seem right. The electric tension was in the air. I told my homeboy, "If we can't find a Mazda or Toyota, this dent puller isn't going to work. We're gonna have to do what we're gonna have to do. We need this car." Then my homeboy responded, "Don't trip. We're gonna get this bad boy one way or another."

There was no Mazda or Toyota in sight. We walked past La Posta. That led us down to Wightman Street where we found the car we'd been looking for. We tried to dent pull it. It didn't work.

CHAPTER 2

We tried to hot wire it. Normally this kind of thing would take us 30 seconds. Time kept ticking away. Suddenly, we saw a man with a crowbar coming toward us at full speed. He yelled, "Get out of that car before I beat you." This man didn't know the state of mind that we were in.

We were high on crystal meth and not thinking rationally. In our mind, he was the bad guy. The man had every right to be angry. We were messing with his property. In my state of mind, I felt threatened, so the man was shot one time.

After the shot was fired, I ran for my life. Beads of sweat trickled down my face. Each bead felt like every year that would be taken from my life. The adrenaline pumped 1,000 mph. Somebody called the cops. Quickly, a police cruiser pulled up. I ran for my life. Huffing and puffing with no place to hide. The ghetto bird circling in the air. Now there would be no chance for escape. I got away for a few seconds but the pursuit was at full force. At two in the morning, I was running down University Avenue and cut the corner on Cherokee Avenue. Out of the corner of my eye, I saw some hidden blue dumpsters. I quickly jumped inside. It felt like an inferno. Sweat was pouring. Flashes of police lights creeped into the smelly dumpster. Barks of K9 rang into the hollow trash can. Creepy shepherd dogs with their nostrils and fangs open, saliva dripping from their mouths like hungry wolves.

I felt the aura of lost years in that tight fitting blue dumpster. It was the darkest moment in my life. The heavy lids swung open. Bright lights shining on my blinded eyes. A mad dog jumped in and began to bite my leg. I struggled with the dog while the police pounded me with batons. I was dragged out and beaten over and over. Then, I was shoved into the back of a cop car, with steel mesh separating the front from the rear. I was hurled into the fetal position with hand cuffs on. The police car sped away with me in the back seat. The pain from the beating down made my whole body ache. That was the least of my problems. I landed in the San Diego county jail with a black eye, busted lip and sore bones. Worst of all, I was facing charges of attempted murder. With nowhere to hide. This is where my prison career began.

As mentors, we know now that exposure to community violence has been linked to increases in aggressive behavior and depression regardless of prior experiences or symptoms (Ford, Chapman, Connor, & Cruise, 2012). Youth who have grown up in contexts of chronic poverty and community violence often yield overall higher scores on measures of trauma symptomatology.

Reader Reflections

If you don't have a father in your home, who is your male guidance?

_____

_____

_____

_____

_____

Are you open to allowing a positive support system in your life?

_____

_____

It's okay to having a lot of energy. Are you channeling it in a positive way? How?

_____

_____

_____

_____

_____

Who do you look up to and why?

_____

_____

_____

Criminal Addictive Behaviors

The fish tank in the old San Diego County jail was flooded with individuals facing long prison terms. The three strikes law was in full affect. The system was handing out life terms like it was the thing to do. At age eighteen, I felt afraid, in a sea with live sharks and nowhere to hide. Something inside of me felt like I had done something really wrong. My conscience began to get the best of me and I felt lost. I didn't know what to expect. Juvenile Hall was one thing. The pipeline to prison was another. I was the youngest kid there.

The tank was disgusting. The shoe wars were a reality. Every man had to protect his own. I remember calling my mother with my free phone call. She answered the phone, "Hola." I felt a big hole in my heart. I felt this big letdown of guilt taking over me and my lips quivered, "Hola. I messed up Ma. I don't know if I'm ever coming home now. I'm sorry. I have all kinds of charges and I'm in the San Diego County jail." She yelled at me for a very long time. Then the howling and weeping began. A mother's pain is so frightening. Hurting the mother you love is the worst feeling

"Why? God! Why?" she cried. I listened with a whirlwind of emotions and tears ran down my cheeks. They ran down too many more holes in my heart. More holes I was creating. Then in my mind I had an image to portray. Somehow, I got it together. I was forced to deal with the realities that were in front of me. It was time to pay the price for my actions.

During the police pursuit, I'd lost my white Nike Cortez tennis shoes. After a couple days in the disgusting fish tank, I landed in the South Bay county jail. They housed me in high power because of the charges I was facing. A three-man cell with three metal bunks. Two adults and me. The tank was cleaner and I had a few homeboys from my area there. The men in my cell were facing the three strikes law. Most everyone was. The mentality was that no one had anything to lose. That extreme-thinking can cause a lot of havoc. Right away, one of them said, "Why are you here? Where are you from? Where is your paper work?"

I had to answer up. I had no choice in the matter. There were rules I now had to abide by. I told them where I was from and gave them the paperwork of my charges. Their demeanor changed. A warm welcoming began to take place. "Don't worry about it youngsta. You're good. Don't sweat it. You have a few homeboys here from your area. They're going to look out for you."

My cellies (cell mates) put a care package together. Relief flowed over me. The man-to-youth guidance began to take its role. The father figure role relationships began to build. The scary thing is that the role modeling came from adults with criminal minds.

The bruises were going down and I felt dirty. I needed a shower. Fortunately, we were going to be let out into the dayroom. In the dayroom, I began to see familiar faces. Homeboys from the area ran up to me with big smiles. They shared hugs and love. I looked up to them. My sense of belonging was present again. One of them, who had just been in my neighborhood before incarceration, was facing life as well. He ran up to me and said, "What's up foo'?" I gave him a big hug and was so excited to see him.

"What's krackin'?" he asked. "Man, I messed up. I'm through. I have all sorts of charges pending."

I said, "I heard. We're in the same boat." He stared at the brown county-issued sandals on my feet and made a beeline to his cell. He came out with some brand new white Reebok classic sneakers and yelled, "Put these on foolio!" I could feel the love. He was a few years older than me. That same day, I got moved to a cell with two of my neighborhood's homeboys. The war stories began and now we could talk in confidence. We would escape in conversation.

Then the reality of the court system hit. On my first court date, I met my lean public defender, who wore bottle cap glasses. I pleaded not guilty to all charges. I had the opportunity to get a quick glimpse at my mother sitting in the court. My heart dropped.

That day, an attorney visit was scheduled. He came to the county jail the next day. The code of honor was for me never to snitch anyone out. In my young mind, I decided to take full responsibility. I took the wrap on my transcripts. So, the evidence against me was stacked up strong.

There was a connection at my attorney visit. The lawyer talked to me as if I was a kid. I really was. I was completely lost for direction. Before we even got to the case, I remember telling him a story about Arizona Boys Ranch and how proud I was to have run the Long Beach Marathon and my mother being there at the finish line. Marathon running is what he did as well. So the connection came with empathy. He climbed into the hole I was in and told me, "Even though your case is not looking good, I am going to give it my best effort. I talked to your mom and she is so worried about you. She thought she could hire private contractors to come and protect you in here. She is a great woman and she is praying for you." I said, "Tell my mother I love her and that I am sorry for all the pain that I have caused her."

On that visit, we didn't talk about the case much. There was so much evidence against me. So his best option was to get the best deal he could for me not to get three strikes or a life term. We talked about all sorts of topics. The man was cool. I had confidence that he was truly going to try his best.

I came back to the tank and shared all that with my cellies. They were all negative and had a lot to say about public defenders and the judicial system. A few weeks passed and my readiness appearance came. The moment of truth. The time for the public defender, the district attorney and the judge to try to reach a plea bargain. At this time, life terms were a norm. The three strikes campaign was on fire. There was zero tolerance.

After the wheeling and dealing, my public defender came into the holding tank where I was shackled from head to toe. He told me, "I have a great deal for you. This is the best it's going to get." I was excited and responded, "What is it? What is it?" He looked me straight in the eyes and said, "Seventeen years with half time and one strike. It's the best it is going to get and if we don't take this deal now, we're not going to get it again. The only reason they are giving it to you is because you were honest about taking responsibility and because of your young age."

I didn't know what to think. For some reason, I thought

from our visits that this man was just going to get me out and make this all go away. I asked him, "What does my mom think?" He responded, "She thinks you should take the deal."

One of the biggest decisions I would have to make in my life. Seventeen years was too much for me. I couldn't see the light at the end of that dark tunnel. But I took my mother's advice. I took the deal and signed all kinds of paper work. Now the sentencing lay ahead. I still couldn't grasp this reality. It seemed like an eternity. It felt like someone chocked me and took my life away. I remember the ride back to South Bay county jail as the chains on my hands and feet jingled on the Sheriff's bus. I stared out at the city of San Diego. I remember thinking this is my last time seeing the outside world. But I still had one more court date.

The day of sentencing came—the day the deal would be finalized. I still had some hope that somehow, some way, I would be cut free. Once again, I saw my public defender and my mother quietly sitting in the court. I said a small prayer to God, hoping that He would create a miracle. I can remember this day so vividly. I went up with my lawyer before the judge. Then the judge began to ask me questions about all different codes and acceptance of plea bargains. I said yes in response to everything but my mind was in a daze. Then the judge sentenced me to seventeen years in a California State Penitentiary with one strike. Right after his words came out with my sentence, my suffering mother screamed and cried. The howls made my brain shake with emotion and the tears ran down my face. I looked over to her and saw the deputies attempt to comfort her but the cries continued. To me, it seemed like an eternity. Then back to the county jail I went, with my mother's screams rattling in my head.

CHAPTER 2

Upon arrival in the jail, my new network of support attempted to console me but I went back to my cell alone reminiscing about all that I would lose. I took a glance at a card that my mom had mailed me with Bible verses printed on it, and suddenly a gush of tears came over me. I was going to be gone for a very long time.

I landed in Centinela State Prison, level 4, C yard. I was in 4 block. The San Diego Chargers were playing against the 49ers at the Super Bowl. My new cellie and I watched the Super Bowl on the dayroom television. Although TVs were allowed in cells, we were just getting there and getting situated. My cellie had been to prison before but I had not. I had a bald head with no facial hair. I still looked about sixteen years old, the youngest kid on the yard. More than half the population there was doing life terms or extended prison terms.

On my first day on the yard, it felt like a huge park with no life in it. It had a big running track with iron weights. At that time, weights were still allowed in California prisons. The division of race was obvious. African Americans had their side of the yard and the Mexicans and Latinos had their own too. Politics were firm. If you didn't abide by the rules, you were at risk of getting stabbed. The yard at that time would "go down" every few days, meaning there was an incident. Most of the time, the "meat wagon" (emergency medical technicians) would come out and take the victim to the hospital. There was either a stabbing or razors to the neck. The yard had no conscience and I was the youngest kid there. The male-to-male guidance went to another level. I was taught how to sharpen knives, be on my toes and always defend the code of honor. The code of honor to my Mamita was one thing but in prison it was a whole different ball game. Convicted criminals had a lot of hostility and emotions built up. In prison, there is nothing better to do than to plot and scheme and get high.

The years flew by and I learned every criminal behavior there is to know. I was also involved with them. A trip to the AD SEG (administrative segregation) was the norm. At age eighteen, I was introduced to shooting up heroin. The first time it made me feel sick. After that it took all my pain away. My criminal mind started to become like the influences around me. I needed someone to look up to. These role models taught me that extreme thinking is the path to follow. Within five years, the state prison placed me in the SHU (segregated housing unit) and I was no longer allowed on the main line because of criminal behavior. However, the family support was always there. Their love is what brought me home.

I went to Corcoran State Prison SHU for a few months before I got transferred to Pelican Bay State Prison SHU. During the time I was in Pelican Bay SHU, the program and routine never varied. I was in an eight-cell pod. Other than the fellow convicts in the pods, no other human contact was possible. Everyone's skin was pale from the lack of sunlight. The rooms were inflexible. The Pelican Bay SHU had a music all of its own. Opening and closing of electronic doors, the day and night conversations, TVs echoing, the clash of trays at meal time, the shuffles of slippers on the cement floor at shower time. The pod felt like a big bubble floating into outer space. A space ship gliding throughout the universe.

It was an environment of isolation and an aura of intense hate toward authority. Nevertheless, we were surrounded by sharp individuals. That's where my intense reading and self-education began. I read hundreds of books and took college courses while I was there. That was my way of escaping the four corners of my cell. I was a prisoner of the Pelican Bay torture treatment. But in my mind, I was at ease knowing that I had the opportunity of a parole date. Eighty percent of SHU inmates had life sentences. Some were gang members with beautiful minds, with enough knowledge to have the capability to be teachers, businessmen and scientists. Entrepreneurs are the risk takers in life. Convicts are also risk takers. The criminal only displays it in a different manner. If they are able to correct their criminal behaviors and transfer themselves to something beautiful these individuals can be productive members of society.

I stayed busy, so I wouldn't lose my mind. The hardest criminals could be the softest. Oprah Winfrey was one of the most touching parasocial influences in our lives. We loved her and she made us feel good about ourselves. She would inspire us to have good conversations about good things that were happening in our communities. Her heart was pure and inspired us to be better people.

Routines made time fly by faster. I received one visit from my family while I was in Pelican Bay SHU. I told them it was too far away, so not to visit me. They came to visit me on my last year of my parole date. During that year, my mind was racing and I had all kinds of ideas. I shared some of my mind with the people in the pod. But I felt guilty in my heart. So I didn't share too much more because most of these men were never going to get out. So, I kept most of my exciting emotions to myself. Time flew and my parole date came in 2007. God had granted me another release date.

Reader Reflections

If you relate to this story, why do we hurt the people we love?

_____

_____

_____

The quick excitement behavior. Is it worth sacrificing your freedom for it?

_____

_____

Are you trying to be a part of the system all of your life?

_____

_____

_____

Stripping down every day. Is that a comfortable feeling for you?

_____

Instead of being destructive in your community, how can you be productive?

_____

_____

_____

_____

_____

CHAPTER 2

Ride or Die

Finally, the day came, after almost fourteen long years, on a layover at Donovan State Prison in San Diego. My parole officer came to pick me up. My family was not allowed to pick me up at the prison gates because of my high control status. I had a box of brand new parole clothes that my mom had sent me. My heart was beating 100 mph. Freedom to me used to be an abstract word. Now it was physical, tangible, something to enjoy and savor. Freedom meant breathing fresh air, eating what you please and, most importantly, being with the ones you love. I was smelling good and looking sharp. My parole officer took me straight to the Glass House (a recovery house) in Chula Vista and took pictures of every inch of my body while asking what each tattoo meant.

On the way to my mother's house, he asked me, "Do you want a burger from McDonalds?" I said, "Why not?" My nervous system had already gone haywire. I could feel the dried up sweat on my body. It began to get worse. The rest of the car ride was silent. Then we arrived at my mom's home in southeast San Diego. I stepped out of the car and my mother was there to greet me with her husband, Mr. Wales, and my two sisters. The feeling was awkward. Then my mom gave me a great big bear hug. Our tears began to pour out with happiness. The parole officer sped off and I began to enjoy my freedom with my family. I felt so nervous; I didn't know how to act. I couldn't sleep for two days straight. This was a whole new world to me. It was not something I was used to. In prison I was told it would take me like 30 days to adjust back into society.

Time flew by quickly. I spent the first day with my family.

My lovely mother that I would die for in her upper 50s but still strong and commanding, with a huge heart. A strong character with tremendous energy. The only woman that stood by me during my darkest years. My number one woman. A mother's only son, a love that could never be challenged. Even though she would never say, "I love you." It was just not part of her character. But deep down I know she loves me with all her might and soul. All the headaches that I put her through. My mother was there through thick and thin.

I was so excited to be out. It was the beginning of my new life. Two weeks out, I was already on a job hunt. Everyone thought I should relax and not worry about rushing to work. In my mind, the job was more for staying preoccupied. By staying busy, it would keep me out of the spotlight. I was a branded man with a target on my back, on high control parole with a CDC number over my head. According to the statistics, I was part of a mass incarceration cycle in which I would end up back in prison. Since childhood, I'd always had a determined work ethic. Whether it was legal or illegal, I put in my best effort. The line that a felon can't get a job is somewhat true. For me, it took two weeks and I got myself a job at a manufacturing warehouse called Frazee Inc. I was hired on the spot as a laborer through a temp agency.

A few months out, I realized life was a blessing but not easy. In prison, everything was handed to me. It gave me a place to lay my head and three meals a day. However, the trade-off was nothing close. I am the type of individual whose mind continually runs. Criminal thoughts would come into my brain and haunt me at times. I stayed focused and worked six days a week. I had time for nothing else. Nine or ten months passed and the thought came into my head, "I've been away so long, let me try to catch up with lost time." So I connected back to the people I knew and the neighborhood where I was from. I was given a lot of love and attention from individuals that I grew up with. Especially a lot of attention from the new generation. I was getting free clothes and free jewelry. I felt the love but it was connected to criminal behaviors.

Shortly after that, I was partying hard every weekend. That left me open to my old behaviors. The wicked drug of crystal meth was out destroying the community as always. I had a taste and before you know it I was trying to work, smoke, and trying to catch up with lost time. One time I was pulled over on Willie James Jones and Imperial Avenue on a routine traffic stop. I was high on crystal meth. I knew they would tear the car upside down. To get away, I swallowed an 8 ball of crystal meth (3.5 grams) and I was on my way to the county jail. They did a parole search of my apartment and I ended up getting two violations. Gang association and drug paraphernalia.

On the way to county jail, the police officer said, "I saw you swallow something. It's not worth your life man." I responded, "I don't know what you're talking about." In my mind, it was well wrapped. I got processed in a new jail. Fifteen years later, and the process hadn't changed. In the holding tank, I made calls and started reaching out. I called my mom. I fed her a lie or two: That everything was going to be alright. I called the homeboy of mine that had wrapped up the wicked drug and he told me that it was not wrapped up good. I didn't think anything of it. My mind was still going 100 mph with the crystal meth.

Then an hour later, I could feel something in my stomach bubbling. The acid in my stomach was eating up the plastic wrapping on the drug I swallowed. I started getting paranoid and I knew something was not right. Suddenly, a rush began to come over my head. The crystal meth package was exploding in me. A week before, I had heard of someone overdosing on crystal meth and the drugs ate up the person's brain. I knew I needed oxygen to my brain. I called my mother and told her, "I love you mom," and she said, "I love you too mijo." In a matter of a minute I lost control. I couldn't even see straight. I was walking from side to side. I could see the nurse walking down the hall. I remember yelling to her, "I'm over dosing on crystal meth and I need oxygen to my brain!" That's the last thing I remember. It was a Friday evening. I woke up on a Tuesday evening to a panel of doctors talking over me. They told me I had crystal meth in me. My response was, "I don't know what you're talking about." After they had saved my life, I was still in denial.

The sad part of this situation is that my mother was notified that I was in there. She went to go pick up my property from the county jail and they informed her that I was in the hospital. She rushed over there with her husband Pastor Ed Wales. They only had 10 minutes. My mother said my eyes were closed but I was swimming around with my arms and legs. I had IV tubes all over me and my mother thought the cops had beaten me and put me in this position. Pastor Wales took advantage of the opportunity and clung on to me and wept and cried to God for my life, so that God could create a miracle. After the ten-minute visit, they notified my mom of the truth. They told her, "Your son swallowed crystal meth and he was overdosing." The cops did not do anything to him. She felt more pain that this wicked drug had caused this to her son.

After my hospital stay, I was sent back to the county jail.

Then I went to Donovan State Prison for a six-month parole violation. Acquainted with old criminally minded friends, I knew that nothing productive was going on. In my mind, I thought I was slick. I escaped death. I got away with just violations and I would be out again to live my life. My problem was that the criminal mindset had become part of my everyday thought process. It was at an all-time high. Getting out, I went right back to the crowd I was hanging with when I violated parole. I was out for three months and caught a ten-month violation. I was addicted to crystal meth and the in-and-out cycle began to take over my life. My criminal addictive behaviors were my number one priority. I felt trapped. Deep down, I was a good person. I wanted more out of life, but at this point I didn't know how to get it.

I was at an all-time low in my life. I would go to church every now and then to make my mother happy. But I was a lost soul. A few years passed and I was starting to get tired of the same old cycle. Then I one day, I went to a trap house and I ran into this thin, brown skinned, beautiful lady with freckles, named Gabby. She caught my attention immediately and I reached out to her with the best game I had. I told her, "My mom has a home that houses people with mental behavioral challenges and I'm not too good at this Craigslist thing on the computer. Do you think you can help me? I'm trying to get some furniture and stuff for the home these people are in." She seemed doubtful that I did not know my way around a computer. I really didn't but at the moment that was my way to get her engaged in conversation. It worked.

She came to my house and never left after that. The computer line worked. At first, she said, "I just want to be your friend." I was cool with that. We were lost in our addiction for the months to follow, hustling every day and living the criminal lifestyle. During this process, we began to have feelings for each other. I asked her to be my girl and she said, "Yes." From that moment on, she was my "Ride or Die". We purposely never left each other's side. I didn't know too much of my girlfriend's history. I knew she had two kids but she didn't talk much about it. We were both running from our realities with shame and guilt from all the pain and suffering we had caused people. On her Facebook page, I was able to see the good life she once had. We started having conversations about our families and what we were doing was not right. We needed to change our lives. We both agreed that there was more out of life than this type of lifestyle.

The seeds of love for each other began to bring out good things. We wanted change. We just didn't know where to start. So we went about our daily lives. We got arrested together soon after that and went to the county jail together. Upon release, I was mandated to an inpatient program at Volunteers of America. Gabby needed a place to get clean if we were going to make this relationship work. I took her to my mom's and told my mom, "I love this woman. Please help her." My mom finally agreed. She has a great heart. The journey to recovery began.

Every day at my program, I got a two-hour pass and Gabby would come every day to downtown on her bicycle or the trolley. She would bring food and we would have little picnics. That's when I started realizing that this woman could cook! Her love for me was pure. Now that we were clean, we could feel the good emotions inside ourselves. We started dreaming together. We wanted this or that out of life and the number one core value that we had was family. We wanted our families' trust back. Four months into our fresh recovery, we had the kids back with us, a house and a nice car. Life was going great. We were going to church to let our presence there be felt but we weren't fully committed. That left us open and vulnerable to attacks from the devil.

Unfortunately, we had a two-week relapse that took us downhill fast. Before we knew it, we ended up in the county jail again. The devil attacked us strong. The crystal meth drug is not to be played with or used recreationally whatsoever. For all of you that have shared these type of experiences, don't you want to change for the better?

This time I was at my all-time low. Total distrust from my family. I lost my home, the kids went back with their grandma and I was away from the woman who I loved. This was a different type of low for me. I came in to county jail with just a violation but in a matter of minutes it turned into five different charges. I came in with some crystal meth again and they found it. I had charges pending that could put me away for 10 years plus. I remember going to my cell and looking out the dayroom window and I asked myself, "Is this the life that I want? Do I want to live like a dog in a cage?" In my cell, I got on my knees and I cried out to God. "I'm done! I need help! I tried it my way and it didn't work out. I surrender." For some reason, I felt peace. I had everything stacked against me but I knew that finally I was on the right track. Everything was in God's hands. My girl and I were together but needed to be away from one another to get our minds right. She bailed out, but she was still in her addiction for a few more weeks. We talked over the phone, and I said to her, "There is only one way. That crystal meth needs to be behind us and we need to be committed to God. Are we in this together or not? I don't know what I'm facing but we'll leave that up to God to decide." She responded, "I love you. We're going to get through this. I'm going to my mom's house tonight and I'm going to start getting my life right for me and my kids; and when you get out, God willing, we will have a strong foundation." We were serious about our commitment.

Shortly after that, I went to court with peace in my heart. I was given the best deal I could get. A flat sixteen-month prison sentence. I thank God for that. My journey of recovery began. In the county jail and prison I was offered drugs and I declined. Something came over me that I would never touch drugs again. This latest incident made me realize the value of life. I was transferred to Chino State Prison AD SEG. That prison was the ugliest. During the summer, the weather was sticky and nearly everyone there was in a state of depression. I wrote Gabby every day and we motivated one another through letters, pictures and encouraging words. She wasn't allowed to visit me because she was my crime partner in court documents but my girl was there by my side, strong in spirit.

Gabby was mandated to Mental Health Systems for her possession charges. She was in an out-patient program. She got a job within the first two months of being at her mom's. Then right after that, she got us an apartment. Even though I was in prison, I felt this motivating energy that I finally was getting my life together. I was really looking forward to paroling. I would have to prove myself to my mom and family again to really get their trust back. In those sixteen months in prison, I received only one letter and one jpay (money gram for canteen) from my mom. That's when I realized my mother was fed up. She never stopped praying and fasting. She knew God was working his miracles in me. It was only a matter of time.

A hunger strike organized by Chino inmates to get more prison rights was depressing. We were some starving men but it made me realize how much pain and hurt was within those prison walls. I was beginning to work on myself. Everyone in there had similar stories like mine. Being in the hole (AD SEG) gives you plenty of time to think and reflect on your life. I would escape those walls by writing to Gabby.

When I had three months left to my parole date, the C.O (commanding officer) came to my door and said, "It's time for you to pack. You're going to Corcoran SHU." I still owed indefinite SHU time so that's where I would have to finish up. The next morning I was on my way. I remember celling up with a friend of mine from the San Diego county jail. I came across a lot of old acquaintances. I got classified and was approved for the dog cage yard twice a week. I ran into people I hadn't seen in fifteen to twenty years. They were older and grayer. You could feel the pain in their eyes. Ninety percent of the people there where never getting out. It was the same story over and over. "What's wrong with you? What are you thinking? I wish I could have had the chance that you have. Why don't you act your age?" was all I heard from everyone there. I felt a sense of guilt. Because time after time after time I would get opportunity after opportunity. I started telling everybody, "I'm not coming back. I'm done with any type of criminal behavior. I want to live life for you guys. I want to start a family."

The conversations I had were different during this term. I

tried my hardest to not use profanity. I respected everyone. I was just on a different mission. I had many one-on-one conversations with lifers. Heart-to-heart talks. I guarantee you that if they were blessed with the opportunity of a parole date, they would never come back. The reality of having a life term hanging over you can really have a mental effect on you. A parole date would be a fresh start to a new life. To everyone that I have done time with throughout the state of California: I love you all and miracles do happen. I believe in you all and if you get that opportunity to fly away from the prison walls, do the right thing. My wife, community mentors and I are examples that it can be done. Don't let anyone tell you different. Dreams do come true.

Corcoran SHU was also a reality check for me. I never want to see that place again or any prison for that matter. Unless it's to go in there to help and support and uplift the individuals that I have been able to relate with all of my life.

A week prior to paroling, I was transferred back to Donovan State Prison in San Diego to parole. I remember reading, "The Purpose Driven Life" by Rick Warren and I prayed every day for Jesus to protect me and my family. The day finally came. My probation officer came to pick me up and took me to the Light House recovery home in the city of El Cajon. I filled out paperwork and they told me that I would be going to an MHS program. It was mandated for six months. I was a little bummed out but I was so excited about being out. The first chance I got, I took advantage of it. I asked the secretary if I could call my girl and let her know that I'm out. She said, "Sure." Right away, I dialed Gabby's number. I was so excited that I got nervous and my words didn't come out as I thought them. A lot of built up emotions. I had not heard her voice in months.

I was then driven to the apartment that my girl had already gotten for us. She and the kids came downstairs to greet me. We hugged and we kissed. I remember thinking, I'm not going to let myself and our family down. My girl had done a great job. A nice apartment in Golden Hills. The furniture was nice. We all were just happy to be together. Our parent journey began.

Reader Reflection

How much pain can you keep inflicting on the ones you love?

_____

If something is not working in your life, why not change it? Who or what might motivate you for healthy change?

_____

_____

How do you learn to love yourself again?

_____

Can you say you are in a healthy relationship?

_____

_____

_____

Is your support system healthy?

_____

_____

_____

_____

How do you think you could commit to change?

_____

_____

_____

_____

_____

CHAPTER 2

A Mother's Intercessory Prayer
(Aleyda Wales)

I lived in an apartment complex in front of Hoover High. There my son, Arthur, who was thirteen at the time had a friend with a troubled family. They influenced him to run away from home. They would make him drive a car because all of the family had a bad track record and couldn't get a driver's license. When he got up at 1 a.m. and left, he went to a foster care placement facility. He said he was abused by his mom and that's why he was looking for somewhere else to live. At 3 a.m. I got a call from the police.

"Are you Arthur Soriano's mother?" they asked. I said, "Yes." They then said, "Your son is here." So I told them, "No, my son is in bed." They said, "No, he is here with us." So, I went to the room to check if he was there, with the phone in my hand. It looked like he was there, until I moved the blankets and I got upset and yelled, "My son is not here!" So confused as I was, I jumped in my car and went to the address they'd given me. When I got there, they asked me if I knew that my son was on drugs. I said, "No."

That was the beginning of my new tribulations. Soon after, he started to attend Hoover High School. Around this time, he would leave home for a week. When he came home, he was all beaten up. I was naive to this at first until Hoover called home and wanted to meet. This is where I learned that my son was a gang member. He was deep in the gang life by then.

I thought that if we moved, this would stop. Little did I know, we moved to a worse area, with more gang and drug activity. When we moved across the street from Highland Park, he started to run around with men and sell drugs with them. A lot of people would tell me they'd seen my son either all drugged up or drunk. By this time, I no longer slept in my bedroom. I would fall asleep waiting for him in the living room, hoping he would come home. I went to a friend completely desperate, not knowing what to do. She told me to file a runaway report. So I started to do that. After about ten runaway reports, I saw no results. I dropped to my knees and told God, "I give my son to you."

I had a guy who rented a room in my house at the time. He owned a bike. Arthur asked him if he could borrow the bike. He lent it to my son. I saw this as the perfect opportunity to put a stop to this. So I told the guy who lived there to report his bike stolen. This was the first time he went to juvenile hall. He yelled at me, telling me I was a horrible mother. "What type of mother calls the cops on her own son?!" I felt so much pain, but at the same time I saw it as my only solution.

My first time visiting Arthur in juvenile hall was a very emotional day for me. I had so many mixed emotions. But God gave me peace and from that moment on I said, "God, thank you for giving me peace and please give me victory." Then the trend started and just got deeper and deeper. My son was in and out of juvenile hall, doing drugs, gang banging and being a menace to society. One day I heard of a big gang fight incident on Euclid and University Avenue at a Quincenera. Somebody got shot and my son ended up with nine staples on the back of his head. It came out on the local news. God protected him once again.

Then came the biggest shock of my life when he ended up

at the San Diego county jail just after his 18th birthday. I cannot put into words the overwhelming feeling that I had knowing that my son was in an adult jail looking at 25 to life. When I left the courtroom, on my way home, I bought a gallon of water, locked myself in my room for seven days fasting and praying. I asked God, "Please give my son another chance." When his sentencing came up, God answered my prayers. He was given 17 years, with half time.

I thank God because I know that my son did need to be there but not forever. In 1994, Arthur landed in a maximum security prison. In 1993, my new husband Ed Wales and I were blessed with twin girls. My twins and I began to visit my son every weekend. My three kids now began to make memories together. The visiting room was precious to me because it was time when I got to enjoy the laughter of my kids together. But the process to get to that point was a lot of work and sacrifice. My son would smile and he would eat up twenty dollars of quarters on hot wings.

As the years passed, he would transfer from prison to prison, ending up further and further away each time. After six years, I would only get to see my son through thick glass. His contact visits were taken away. I don't know what type of problems he got into but he was always in trouble. I remember on my twins' 14th birthday, I asked them what they wanted for their birthday. They both said they wanted to see their brother. By this time, he had been at Pelican Bay State Prison SHU for the past four years. When we went to see him, I looked up as he was coming down the hall, barely able to walk because of the chains that bound his hands and feet together. He was pale as a ghost. It hurt so bad I let out a yell of desperation and began to cry. I felt so hopeless.

Nine months later he finally got out. I thought all would be better now. I was wrong and the trials and tribulations started again. In the years to come, he was in and out of jail and prison over and over and over. In the process of him being lost in addiction and a criminal lifestyle, he met his wife Gabby. All I could do was continue to pray. I waited for God to grant me a miracle. It finally happened when my son was 37 years old and decided to change his life.

When I first met Gabby, she was lost in her addiction and lifestyle too. I told her she was not for my son and Gabby told me she loved my son and was not going anywhere. Sometime after all their ups and downs, my son got out of prison for the last time. They both began to attend church and God answered all my prayers.

To all mothers who read this book, please don't lose hope. God is the only one that can change anybody. Continue to support your children with prayer and give them to Jesus Christ.

CHAPTER 2

Gabby's Mom's Perspective
(Modesta Hernandez)

Gabby is the fourth of five children. She began misbehaving with so-called friends, experimenting with drugs and running the streets. I remember showing up at her school to pick her up and at times she was not there. She would leave with her friends. They would go lock themselves in a friend's garage and smoke marijuana. Her life would at times be good and at times not. She had a baby and was doing well for some time afterwards. She was a good hard-working single mother. But then came across some more bad influences and left her son with me for days at a time. She went back to her addiction as I took care of her son. Some years later she had a baby girl and did well for some time after that. Then she fell right back into that negative lifestyle. She would leave her two kids with me off and on throughout the years.

For the most part, she was a great mother and would provide for her kids. She had lots of ups and downs until she met Arthur. They met while running the streets. I then told God that I didn't have any more strength and asked God to please not close his hands until she was in them. She continued to do bad and once again left her kids with me again. No one could imagine a grandmother's suffering, seeing those innocent children and hearing them cry and ask for their mother. I had to ask God for forgiveness for lying to them and telling them their mom was working and she'll be home soon. The days would pass and I just kept praying to God. One day, she came back home and asked me for forgiveness and I told her, "God bless you." She left. I didn't know where she was staying.

God led her down a Christian path. She was still seeing Arthur. My prayers led her to Aleyda Wales (Arthur's mom). By God's grace Aleyda helped Gabby get clean and live in an environment that instilled the same rules and Christian ways which I always showed her. Arthur and my daughter both got it together and established a healthy life together. They got engaged and began going to church. They rented their first place together. All was going well and they had the kids with them. The kids were happy again and they had their home. God blessed them with a home, a car and work. They were set.

Then they forgot about God's favor and grace. They began to rely on themselves instead of God and they foolishly began to think, "I can, I know." Again, the two of them went back to jail. Again, the kids were let down. She got out on bail and kept going to church with her kids. When Arthur got out again they continued that healthy relationship they once had. They got married and God forgave them and blessed them with a son.

I am so happy to say that they now have been attending church for some time and they actively serve the community too. Now, Arthur's mother and I give all glory to Jesus Christ. Every day we thank God. So, to all readers and mothers, this has been a mix of sadness, joy and happiness. It has been about always continuing in God's path. These are the answered intercessory prayers of a mother.

Reader Reflections

A mother's love is pure. Why would you do things to hurt them?

_____

_____

_____

_____

When was the last time you did something great for you mom?

_____

_____

_____

Community Therapy Community Mentors
(Arthur Soriano)

I came home to my beautiful wife, Gabby Soriano, and our two kids. They were healing from their trauma and then I came into the picture. I was embraced and felt the genuine love from all. Gabby was already sixteen months clean. She had completed her drug program at MHS and was going to church. She was strong and created a strong foundation for us. I was blessed to have her in my life. The parenting journey began. Ultimately, I give God the glory and the honor for putting me through all the trials and tribulations I had been through. Now, I truly felt he had a purpose for my life.

I was done. My path to total transformation was starting. I was on probation. I was mandated to go to a program on El Cajon Boulevard called MHS. At first I was frustrated that I would have to go through this process. I had already given my life to God. Why did I have to do this? I surrendered myself to the process and went through the program. I knew I would have to get past this stepping stone to get to where I needed to go.

My first day there, I ran into my homeboy named Juan Valderrama. I was excited to see him. He told me he was graduating in a couple of weeks. I could tell he was sizing me up to see where my head was at. All he knew was I was fresh out. He couldn't tell if I wanted a different life or not. We only knew one life together, so this was awkward and different. He gave me some advice on how to complete the program and the rules and regulation. I could tell he wanted change but we didn't get too deep into the conversation. I was happy for him that he was graduating. It gave me some hope about the process. We agreed that we were going to stay away from one another. Right now wasn't the time to hang out. We needed to work on ourselves.

My first step was to get off probation. To do that, I needed to complete the program. That was goal number one. That would take from six to eight months, so I decided to put my full effort into a six-month plan. I would go to church two times a week, then three times a week to MHS, and also I would attend four Narcotics Anonymous meetings each week. I was working for my Mother Aleyda Wales, now founder of Mi Casa Es Su Casa, housing individuals with mental behavioral challenges. I was in charge of cleaning the three homes.

My beautiful daughter, Daniella, invited me to her school called McGill School of Success. It was a small school with a big heart. It was Family Friday. That's where my heart of volunteering began. It was a beautiful feeling. Mrs. Delia, her teacher inspired me and motivated me to be involved. I didn't miss a Friday. Before I knew it, I was doing the spelling tests with the students and going on field trips. It made me feel like a kid again. Those Fridays were pivotal to my transformation. They made me feel special. We looked forward to Fridays. I am so grateful for that opportunity.

Time-wise, the programs I was involved with were a challenge. I didn't have a car and asking everyone for rides became old. I stood strong. Gabby paved the way. I thought, "If she can do it, so can I." I was in the same group she was in, with the same counselor. What she learned was now being passed down to me. I began to get involved with the groups. Participating and asking questions is key.

Then a curriculum, "Criminal Addictive Thinking &

Addictive Behaviors" was taught in the group. I was so intrigued with it and I paid close attention. I could identify with all the behaviors. If I didn't, I knew a criminal that did. During this process, I learned I was an individual that would get a thrill from quick excitement. I was in it for the moment and wouldn't think of the consequences from my choices. I was trying to catch up with time that I had lost. Guess what? That time was already gone. I was able to identify my core values and what was truly important to me. The core values of the past were no good. They led me straight to prison.

What was important to me? My entire family was important to me. Being a productive member of society was important to me. Not to go back to jail was important to me. Being able to live life was important to me. Being a positive role model was important to me. Being a good dad was important to me. Giving back to my community was important to me. I had true core values now that I would stick by. These were the core values Gabby and I had established.

Blaming the systems was another criminal behavior of mine as well as not taking responsibility for my actions was another trait I needed to work on. Guess what? I might not have had the best of circumstances but ultimately I had a choice. My life was back in my hands and I was planning on taking full control of it. The groups were now exciting to me and I've always loved to learn. I soaked everything up like a sponge. I wanted more out of my life. Those extreme thinking behavioral patterns were no good. I was creating a new thought map that would lead to a road of resilience. I was healing from all my trauma and understanding my way of thinking played a big role in my life.

Every time I checked into probation downtown, I told my probation officer how good I was doing. I had a parole officer called Mrs. Chandler in the past. She was a good person and had seen the good in me. During her supervision of me, I just wasn't ready. However, she was already planting seeds in me, believing that I could succeed. Now, my current probation officer was cool. After three months he told me, "AB 109 is a bit different than parole. If you can give me six solid months without violating, I can get you off the system."

That really fueled my fire. I thought, "It's going to happen!" Every month after that, I always asked, "Can I get off this month? This is what I'm doing in my community. This is the proof. These are my letters of support. I haven't missed one day out of the mandated program. What can I do to serve the people that are in my shoes?"

I love the people I have served and I've wanted to see them break the same chains that I'm breaking. If you're on parole or probation, you have to go in there with a mission-minded mentality that you want this system off your back! Don't hide from them. Be a productive member of society. If they see that in you, that is your best chance. No one wants to be part of the system. What are you going to do to get out of it? BE MISSION MINDED TO DO WHAT'S RIGHT. Trust me, I tried all other paths and it didn't work for me. The criminal lifestyle isn't a career without consequences. Learn from this crash dummy. I've had three convicted arrests and eight to ten violations. That's a proven track record that it doesn't work. Is that the path that you want? Do you want most of your life in the system? I guarantee you, THAT'S NOT WHAT YOU WANT.

Six months passed. My wife and I were married. We made the covenant to be with one another for an eternity. Whoever passes first, the other will be waiting on the other side. We invested time into our relationship to get our lives right. Our story is rare. Relationships don't usually work when the couple have met during their addiction. Our main motto is: "Respect one another." If we get mad at one another, we check in with each other. We give each other a clue that all is good. It's okay to be frustrated. That's part of life.

We had a small wedding with a lot of value in it. We even had a probation raid that day. They rushed into our apartment only to find out we were getting married. Although it was frustrating, the Probation Department knew we were on the right track. All the distrust we had once created because of our addictions was now replaced by a beautiful marriage. I love my wife with all my heart and soul. Our purpose in life during our criminal period was to go through all we went through so we can be healthy parents on a journey with our kids and be community leaders for the individuals that have walked our same paths. That's part of our core values. We want to inspire and motivate individuals to become better people. Whatever their goal is, we want to push them towards that. That's what life is all about.

During this time, my stepson, Adrian, got into an incident at his school one morning. He got the short end of the stick and lost the fight. We received the phone call. Right away, we put the pedal to the metal. The ambulance was there on school grounds. We asked all sorts of questions and our emotions began to get the best of us. Our old behaviors started to surface. Who did this? Where are they at? Our emotions cooled off once we knew Adrian was fine. He was in the ambulance with a busted lip and a few bruises on his face. We all headed to the hospital.

In the emergency room, we supported our son. Five minutes later, two police officers came to find out what happened during the incident. None of us had any information to give them. At first, my criminal behaviors started to resurface. Who is this guy? But after a minute I was convinced that this individual was genuine. I could feel his real intentions. He said, "Adrian, there is a program called "Youth Voice" at the Mid City Police Division. You need to come be a part of it. You're a good kid and this program is going to be a benefit to you. It's every Thursday at 3 p.m."

I responded, "Officer, this is my story. I'm getting my life together and our whole family is in the process of getting it right. I just got out a few months ago. Can I come?" He said, "Sure. There are mentors for the youth there also."

The incident had occurred on a Thursday. Youth Voice was that same day. My wife and our kids went that very same afternoon. Adrian was still healing from his wounds. We still went. Officer John Cooksey's heart was what motivated us. On the way I told my wife, "Baby I don't feel comfortable. I've never been in a police department on my own free will. This is crazy."

She agreed. "Our last incident, we were arrested a few blocks away. I don't trust the system and these people that are involved with them. However, we are here for my son. If this program can work for him. Then, as parents, we have done our job." We took a leap of faith. All was in God's hands.

My nervous system was going haywire the afternoon we walked in to the Mid-City Police Division. My wife and I kept pumping each other with fuel that this was the right thing to do. We walked in there with our heads high. We were embraced by Officer Cooksey, who said, "How are you doing? I'm glad you are here. This is Youth Voice." She then introduced us to Mrs. Dana Brown, and told us, "She is the one that runs the program."

It was October 2014. That's when we met Dana Brown. She loved us. Her heart was genuine and pure. With this soft angel voice, she said, "This is Youth Voice. You are welcome here." We were in a police department. My wife and our son felt the love. Our fears went away. From that day on, we were going to Youth Voice, a new chapter in our lives.

In record time, I was able to get off of probation and complete the MHS program in eight months. It had been a journey from 1991 to 2014. The gorilla was off my back. A day of joy for myself and my family. I was catching momentum. The trust was being gained again from my mother and sisters. I was working, going to church, and staying busy. Life was good and my lovely wife and I were happy.

Dana Brown is such a beautiful person with a big heart. My human angel. Her mentorship and guidance is why I'm here today. She became the inspiration for Youth Empowerment. She challenged me and told me, "What are we going to do to help uplift this broken community in City Heights."

She took me to meetings all around the community, connecting me with leaders so we could come up with solutions.

She was empowering me by believing in me. I felt inspired, so I reached out to Michelle Masset, a friend of mine in the community. She was also with me in the MHS program. We had conversations about being done with the lifestyle. She was going to get her life on track and fight for her kids.

The Community Mentor Movement began. Instead of focusing on all the wrongs in our community, we were focusing on how to make things right. We were connected with the neighborhood, so we wanted to give back to the people we could relate to. Youth Empowerment, is a growing grassroots effort that began by chance when Gabby and I went over to Teralta Park in City Heights looking for a teen we had promised to help mentor, Michelle Masset's son. We found him with a group of others. I joined in for a few pickup games of basketball. Then we talked about life. I told them my story and I caught their attention. We talked about their challenges and their dreams. We were just hanging out. We brought over some pizza and talked. Then when we got ready to leave, the kids were like, "Hey, when are we going to do this again?" I said, "Hey, how about next Sunday?" That was in December 2014. We've made our presence felt at that park ever since.

The word began to spread through the street. More than one-hundred kids, many of whom associate with gangs and almost all of whom are at-risk, have joined the movement that now includes Community Resilience, Community Wraparound, Youth Voice, and Project AWARE. We do fundraising drives for families in need, as well as paintball battles and fishing trips. We take kids to places they have never experienced. The effort has drawn notice from police officers, Juvenile Court judges, city officials and neighborhood activists, as well as families.

"This is the epitome of grassroots, community organizing," said Dana Brown in a City Heights Life article by David Ogul. Dana, a member of San Diego's Commission on Gang Prevention and Intervention who works on a number of related projects in City Heights, said, "Arthur and Gabby are on the ground floor of a phenomenal movement that I really believe can become a national model of an exemplary, replicable program to serve youth who were on a pipeline to prison."

A childhood friend of mine, Robert O, grew up in City Heights. He's the co-founder of Youth Empowerment. Fresh in the movement, he has put in many hours needed to do our best to save these kids' lives. We've spent hours upon hours in the court rooms supporting them and mentoring them. Robert O is the heartbeat of the movement. I appreciate him and his whole family for their time and sacrifice.

Shortly after that, Juan Valderrama Jr., who is a co-founder of Youth Empowerment, jumped into the Community Mentor movement. The last time I had seen him was at the MHS program. We had worked on one another. Now we could begin to give back to the community we had once helped destroy. I appreciate both these gentlemen and all the effort they put into the movement.

Rudy Arias of East San Diego is another founding member. We were in Pelican Bay together for seven years in the SHU (Segregated Housing Unit) in the same block. We were close but yet so far away. We were in different pods and never got the opportunity to see one another personally. He paroled in 2008 at the age of 52 with me. I went through my trial and tribulations. He never turned back. Recently, he gave his life to the Lord Jesus

Christ and he's now part of the Community Mentor Movement. Once a gang leader, he's now giving back to his community with love. That is powerful!

To all the community mentors: I love you all and want to acknowledge you. We are hidden treasures that are going to achieve greatness.

I'm grateful for the opportunity that Alliant University gave us in creating a Community Mentor training program for certification. To Professor Lynn Underwood and Dr. Griffin, I am thankful for your leadership and for the opportunity to bring training to the curriculum at Alliant University. It's a collaborative powerful movement.

During the pilot program, I began to create a more solid relationship with another mentor, Reginald Washington: a hidden treasure in the past. Today he has blossomed into a jewel. Here is his treasure: Project AWARE is part of this beautiful movement. He founded the program in 2003. AWARE is an acronym for Attitude When Angry and Resolving Emotional Issues Non-Violently. As a teenager, Reginald never considered himself to be a violent person, but when he got angry, he did not know how to deal with his anger in a constructive, non-violent way. As a young man, he found himself involved in gangs, without any awareness of alternative peaceful ways to deal with his anger.

He got involved in an altercation one night and shot someone. This resulted in a 14-year-to-life sentence for his crime, and he was forced into a penal system, which did not offer him any rehabilitation; but in fact, thrust him into an increasingly violent setting. He had to learn how to deal with his behavior and emotions or be prepared to spend the rest of his life in prison.

Reginald chose to take back his life by educating himself and becoming more emotionally literate. He worked on his social and cognitive skills and enhanced his problem solving abilities. Over time, he became a facilitator of such programs for creative conflict resolutions and infectious disease education as well as mentoring in a substance abuse program. With the help of those in the San Diego community who believed in him, he began his journey back into society.

Richard J. Donovan Correctional Facility endorses a program called CROP, which stands for Convicts Reaching Out to People. Reginald became involved in this community program that focuses on educating at-risk youth about the behavior that resulted in long prison terms for C.R.O.P. members. He and others produce a program twice a month aimed at helping youth to recognize dangerous activities and make better choices. He was also selected out of hundreds of inmates to become an intern in the HOPE program (a substance abuse recovery program). It was in the HOPE program that Reginald first became involved in a therapeutic community. As he became more educated, he soon realized that sharing himself and his story with others could be a powerful way to help the community.

After spending fifteen years incarcerated in the California Department of Corrections, Reginald was granted parole because he was deemed to be no longer a threat to society due to his ability to accept responsibility for his actions. The AWARE program was created in order to bring something positive to the youth of San Diego from someone who has been there and does not want to see anyone else find out the hard way.

Reginald is certified in several different areas, but it is his life experience that is the heart behind AWARE. The streets of San Diego are filled with angry teenagers who develop gang and substance abuse issues. His vision is to create a place with a climate where young people can learn to communicate and contribute to the overall well-being of their own lives and for those in the community in which they live.

When this first started, all my wife and I wanted was our family to be healthy and on the right path. My daughter, Daniella, got her mother back and a full-time dad in me. Right now, in 2017, she is 10 years old. These are some words she wants to share, "I'm happy to have a family that cares about me. I have a dad that loves me, a mother who cares about me." Short and sweet.

Forgiveness and healing have become a big part of my core values. God works in mysterious ways. In my past lifestyle, I was never ready to be a dad. God waited till I was ready. Then he blessed me with a miracle. Arthur Joshua Soriano Jr. was born a day after my birthday on March 19, 2016. He's the best present I could ever receive and one of the biggest joys of my life. He's my mother's first grandson. This is what I live for now.

The best form of prevention and intervention are healthy parents. The future is bright. We are here to bring out the hidden treasure in YOU. Then you can bring out the hidden treasure in someone else. It'll make the world a better place.

Reader Reflections

When was the last time you volunteered in your community?

_____

_____

_____

What was the last time you showed compassion to another person besides your family?

_____

_____

_____

Are you doing all you can to be a healthy parent?

_____

_____

CHAPTER 2

Isaac Adrian Mejia

"Now that everyone is on the right track, so am I," says, Adrian, Gabby and Arthur's son. "It's like a ripple effect. Now that I'm older and wiser, less stubborn and more humble, I start seeing things for what they really are. I understand why people do the things they do and most of the time it's to escape from reality but when reality hits, it's no longer fun and games. Over the years, I've been arrested for stupid things, brought home by police, also for stupid things. If I had a dollar for every time I chose poorly, I'd be making more money than what me, my mentors, parents, and other family are making currently.

Nothing in life is guaranteed and nobody said it was going to be easy. All you got to do is work for what you want and need. I mean, look at me now. If you compared who I am right now to who I used to be, there would be a major difference. I never cared about school at all, mostly because I was ill-minded. My actions got the best of me and I couldn't help it. But now that everything makes sense, I understand what responsibility, independence and maturity feel like. Now I am a better person.

Ever since I've moved to Garfield High, I haven't been expelled, I haven't ditched, I haven't messed up at all. I went from having straight F's and being below basic to having A's and B's. I'm part of my schools Associated Student Body. I'm taking more classes then I need to be taking (by choice). I got a job, making my own money. I got accepted to San Diego City College, where I start this fall (2017). To top it all off, I never thought I would be doing this, voluntarily.

I'm soon to graduate with my high school class of 2017.

My whole life has been hard because hurt people hurt others, but now that I see the brighter side of what my future is looking like, it's all about healing people.

Arthur Soriano writes: "To hear my step-son say this makes my heart warm. Once Gabby and I got right, then we were able to bring the hidden treasure out of him."

Reader Reflections

How can you find a pathway instead of an escape route?

_____
_____
_____
_____
_____
_____
_____
_____

How can you heal others by healing yourself?

_____
_____
_____
_____
_____
_____
_____

From destructive to productive, how are you going to be productive?

_____
_____
_____
_____
_____
_____
_____

ADVERSE CHILDHOOD EXPERIENCES

CHAPTER 2

Arthur Soriano writes*:*

This is a short story of my sister Rachel Wales lens on my life. I love her and I'm thankful for her forgiveness. She finally was able to see the hidden treasure in me.

Rachel Wales write:s

My twin sister and I were born in 1993. Six months later, my brother was sentenced to 17 years in prison. At the time, I was too young to realize what was going on. As far as I was concerned, my brother was in a place where he wasn't allowed to leave. I remember every weekend going to visit him. The car would overheat. We'd get searched at the prison and stand in lines outside in the hot sun, just to be able to see my brother for only an hour.

I will never forget the first time I saw him through thick glass. Then on later visits, when we would get to the waiting area, I would scan the room and find my brother standing at a table smiling and waving for us to come over to him. One time though, as I scanned the room, he was nowhere to be found, so we had to ask a guard, and he told us he was going to be at the end of the room in the right corner. When we got to where he was sitting, he had one arm cuffed to his hip and the other hand on the phone waiting for us to pick up the other end.

Visits stopped for about five or six years after that. We were told that my brother had been sent to Oregon and it was too far for us to drive.

Four years later, as my sister and I approached our 14th

birthday, we were asked what we wanted. All we wanted was to see our brother. We all decided to give him a surprise visit. At the prison, as we stood in front of the window waiting for him to see us, I was excited and nervous, imagining the look on his face after four years. As I saw him approaching, I went into shock. My brother's hands were cuffed to his hip, his feet were cuffed together and a chain connected his hands, hip and legs. He walked slowly, with his head down and his face was completely pale. My excitement quickly turned to sorrow as I saw the officer uncuff my brother's hands. The wrists were completely red from being cuffed for so long. Instead of smiling and laughing, we all just cried. There were so many stories to be told after four years. An hour wasn't enough.

Then one day, finally, my brother was coming home! I could hug him, talk to him and finally be able to experience what it was like to really have a brother. Unfortunately, for the next couple of years, nothing changed. He still went in and out of prison, rather than living the life I had hoped.

When I was sixteen, I gave up hope. There was no way he was going to change. I was so mad at my mother and sister for still supporting him and standing by his side.

Then when I was twenty years old, the time finally came. My brother changed. It was almost too good to be true. "Was this really happening?" I wondered.

Today I thank God so much that it is finally over. I can honestly say I am proud of my brother. All those years seem like a lifetime ago. He has decided to use his past as a motivation to influence young kids today to do better. I am very happy to have my family back and to know that all those years are being used for positive change.

Chapter 3
Mothers With A Message

Bevelynn Bravo

I grew up in Barrio Logan in San Diego, the youngest of three girls. My sisters were older than me. I don't remember them much growing up. They get upset when I say that because they always had to take care of me when I was little, while my mom worked.

I felt like an only child. My sisters say I was spoiled. My mom called me "Reyna" which means "Queen." She still calls me that to this day. My mother Rosa Maria Rodriguez is from Ixtapa, Ziguatanejo in Mexico. My father Guillermo Losoya Casas was from Chihuahua, Mexico but grew up in El Monte, Mexico. My father brought my mother to the United States with my sisters in about 1962. I was born 11 years later.

CHAPTER 3

My parents separated when I was a toddler. My mom raised me and she was the sweetest mother you could ever be lucky enough to have. She was also the most hard-working lady I have ever known. She always had two jobs.

I lived off Irving Avenue for many years. I loved it there. I grew up playing four square, tag, ring around the rosy, hopscotch, climbing trees, and picking loquat fruit. I always had my hair braided in two pony tails because I had long curly hair and I couldn't have it in my eyes while climbing trees! I had a lot of childhood friends that lived on the same block. We had so much fun playing outside; we never wanted to be indoors. I have nothing but fond memories of my childhood.

I attended Burbank Elementary. The neighbors knew my mother worked and they always looked out for me. I especially remember Mr. and Mrs. Daniels who greeted me when I got out from school. Mr. Daniels would be working in his garden and Mrs. Daniels would have treats ready for me. Then she would tell me to get inside my house until my mom got out of work. Sometimes I would listen. Sometimes I wouldn't because me and my friend Blanca loved going to the neighborhood stores Lucky's or to my friend Teresa's home to buy "Now & Laters" candy." Teresa also knew my mom and she would ask, "Does your mom know you're outside while she's at work?" I would just smile, not really giving an answer because I didn't want to lie but I didn't want to get in trouble either.

I don't know why I worried. I knew my mom wouldn't yell at me or anything like that but I still knew I was not to leave the house while she worked. My mom had so many people looking out for me. Sometimes I wanted to play across the street on the swings but my mom had another friend named Emi, and if she saw me, she would yell my name really loud, telling me to get inside. It was embarrassing. My mom had a friend she worked with, Luz. Luz had a lot of daughters (the Padillas) and they would take care of me too. I had so much fun always surrounded by good people. My mom put me in after-school programs where I would stay until she got out of work. Then later, she put me in magnet programs where I attended school in Ocean Beach. I met a lot of really nice and caring teachers. One was Susie Dyer. She would always say she was my personal cheerleader, and always on my side. She was so fun that groups of us from the after-school program would have slumber parties at her house and make fun arts and crafts while we would share what we wanted to be when we grew up. I wanted to be a veterinarian or a psychiatrist. I wanted to care for sick animals and help them get better. But I also was a good listener because I was quiet. So this drew my desiring also to perhaps be a psychiatrist. I thought it would be wonderful if I could help solve people's problems so they could be happy again. That is what I knew about that profession growing up.

The only thing I did not like growing up was walking! My mom didn't have a car for a couple of years and we walked everywhere. We had to walk to get tortillas. We even had to walk a few blocks to go do our washing and then carry the basket of clothes back home each week. We took the bus when we had to go grocery shopping or to the swap meet. They were a little father distance. I would cry because I was so tired and it was dark by the time we would arrive home. My mom would be so patient and calm, trying to convince me we were almost home.

As I got into my teens, my mom bought a house and we moved to an area of San Diego called Southeast. I did rebel a bit I'm sure. I made my mother cry and worry but my mom was always so loving. I could do no wrong in her eyes and she loved me unconditionally without judgment. It's her love that made me the woman I am today.

At eighteen I was married and had my firstborn, Jaime; he was my pride and joy. I remember my mom and sister taking me to the hospital. I was in so much pain and I was afraid, so I told them to take me home. I was just going to go to sleep and the pain would go away in the morning and I would be fine. The nurses kept telling me that was not a good idea when you're in labor but I went home only to come back again thirty minutes later.

When I first saw Jaime, I could not believe he was mine. I looked at him with such pride and I would always sing the song, "You are my sunshine, my only sunshine, you make me happy when skies are gray." I would also sing, "Heaven must be missing an angel because you're here with me." I loved Jaime with a love I'd never experienced.

A year later, I had my daughter and two years after that, my son. They were perfect and I loved them so much I wanted to give them everything. I was determined to make it. Even though things didn't work out with their father, we were going to be alright. I sent my kids to the best schools, which were out of the area at that time. My children were always involved in camps and activities.

I started working full-time with youth and children at

Homeys Youth Foundation. Soon afterward, I became interested in grassroots and community organizing. I got a job at another non-profit organization, Jacobs Center, where I worked for fifteen years with an amazing group of people.

With the help of my mother I bought my first home. I had remarried at the time and had my fourth child, Little Joe. Life was good and I was faithfully attending church with my children every Wednesday and Sunday at New Harvest and Gateway Christian Church. I would pray every night for my family and would thank God every day for loving me and for everything he'd given me.

My kids had so much love growing up. They had my mom, their grandma, who showed them the love I grew up with. She fed them lobster, shrimp, carne asada, lumpias, pancit, and so much more. "If the kids aren't chunky, they aren't healthy," she would say. They also had my sisters, who were always there to baby-sit, and they had their cousins. We were a small family but close knit.

I worked many hours, dedicating my life to helping people and improving things in my community. I had a saying, "I was always waiting and hoping for someone to come and make some changes in our community. I never knew I was waiting for myself." I loved my job because I got to work with youth everyday. We used to take them to camps and we would have learning exchanges with other community organizers and non-profits around the world. I organized cultural learning exchanges and events so that the kids could learn from different types of people.

We did have crime in our community as well, and we were losing young people. Some of my work was not so fun; it was heart breaking. I became involved in the San Diego Compassion Project, helping families whose sons or daughters were murdered, never thinking one day that would be *me*.

My son's life was taken in 2012. In an instant, my life, the way I knew it, the way my family knew it was gone! I was in disbelief and deep grief. Shortly after that, I lost my job, and shortly after that I lost my house that I had worked so hard for. None of it mattered without Jaime.

Blessings came at the same time. When Jaime's daughter was born six days after he died, I was grieving but joyful at the same time. I had my kids but I was still dying inside. I had enormous support from everywhere. I still remember the day when two detectives came to my house to notify me of Jaime's murder. I told them, "Take me to the scene." I called the executive director of JRYMCA (Michael Brunker) where Jaime had been a junior lifeguard for years. I was in shock and not comprehending everything. I needed help. He got up at 1:30 a.m. to help me. I got to the scene and I stayed there for hours until my son was taken away. I thought I was behind the yellow tape by myself, but every time I looked back, pastors I knew, community members I knew, families I'd helped in the past, friends and family were all there with me in the cold, feeling my pain, grieving with me and my family, showing us their love.

We buried Jaime and I tried my best to trust God and walk in faith. At times, I was so sad, angry, confused; but I didn't want to question God. Even though I was saying all the right things, I was not fully honest with God. One day, my son Little Joe, who was ten years old, came home from school and said, "How long are you going to do this? How long are you going to sit on the couch, cry and look at pictures of Jaime? If you said at the funeral that God is our strength and we have to trust him, why aren't you doing that? I'm just a little kid that still has a long time to live and enjoy life. What about me?" He also told me I was halfway there, that I was closer than he was to being reunited with Jaime. That day I got myself up for my little boy and started to live again for him. I did cry out to God many, many times, telling him to help me through this. Some days, I still would get sad and question God why if I took care of so many others would my son not have been looked after?

Why would this happen to a mother, *me*, who never hurt anyone in her life and always sacrificed for us? I told God, "I am so sad. I miss my son but I still love you. Please help me. I never stopped praying. I also had to be the example for my family. If I didn't make it, they weren't going to make it. I continued helping others; but one day my supervisor Roque Barros said to me, "Bev, you're always helping people bury their kids. What can you do to save them?"

I did not know the answer. His question caught my mind's attention and made me loose sleep. I stayed up many nights thinking about how I could do that. Toward the end of 2012, I founded a group, "Mothers with a Message." Along with a group of other dedicated mothers, we now talk with youth about choices and consequences and a mother's potential lifetime of pain. We also attend curfew sweeps, warning youth about the dangers of being out late. We attend diversion programs and work with youth who might be taking the wrong path. We share our stories in the prisons. We show forgiveness to those who never received it; and in turn we try to be understanding and learn from what happened in their lives, so that we can better help the youth in our communities.

I currently work at UPAC (Union of Pan-Asian Communities) program. I am very fortunate and blessed to work with other earth angels, helping families who have experienced a violent loss. I continue to work with youth through city wrap-arounds and collaborating with the Probation Department to help youth get out of the system. I am in the Chief Probation Officer's advisory board and correctional advisory board.

My purpose here on earth is to give of myself in any way I can in sharing my story to spare someone else my pain and to see youth reach their full potential in life. It was all due to God and the support I received from hundreds of people in my community, people from other cities, other hurting moms before me, my dear friends, my long-time pastor Lou Wilburn, pastors from CAST (Community Assistants Support Team) my fiancé, my family, my kids and the smartest ten-year-old who opened my eyes again. Little Joe, I would not be here without you. I would not have been able to survive after 2012.

Thank you God for when I cried out, "They took my son! It hurts!" You said with love, "I know. They took mine too." I had nothing more to say after that. I just walked in faith.

Chapter 4
Son Of Encouragement

Eric Bruner

I was born in Oklahoma City on August 21, 1978. My mother's name was Wanda Bruner and my daddy's name was Eugene Adams. When I was born, my dad was the only one working in the household. My mom was a stay-at-home mother and I had two older brothers. My brothers' names were Anthony Bruner and Calvin Bruner. We were very poor compared to other families because my dad didn't make that much money. He was only making $3.50 an hour. My dad was also abusive towards my mother. When he used to get upset he would slap, kick, punch and hit her with wet towels. I used to watch my mother crying tears and telling me, "It's okay, baby. Everything is going to be okay." In my mind, I thought that it wasn't okay and I would cry with her.

When I was three years old, my mother got really sick

because of her thyroid problems. The doctor told my mother that she was not going to live past a year. Thank God they fixed the problem and she did not die. After surgery, she came home and noticed that Oklahoma City's electric company had shut off the electricity. Maggots were in the refrigerator, the house was a mess and my dad was nowhere to be found. So my mother took my brothers and me and moved us to Norman, Oklahoma.

In our new city, we felt like we were the only African Americans. My dad didn't know where we went and he went to look for us. All of a sudden, he found us in Norman because a friend of his told him where we were. My dad pulled a gun on my mother and said that he was going to blow her brains out if she didn't get back with him. My mother said, "Okay," out of fear but after he left and went to get his stuff in Oklahoma City, she called the police and filed a restraining order on him. My dad never returned to our lives again.

Our New Life

The apartment that we lived in was a new low-income complex. My mom decided to start hustling, for example selling drugs, stealing, shoplifting and doing drugs as well. I watched her do all these wrong things and was very shocked to see how well she functioned when she was taking care of us. My mom was the dad. She took us to church once a year on Easter, just because she knew of Jesus Christ, but she was not really living for God.

When I was seven years old, I started to stay home by myself. I became very scared and frightened when I didn't see my mother or brothers at home when I arrived back from school. I think at that time, God was showing me that he was with me but I didn't know it because I was so young.

I started to pray because my mother told me to pray. I remember when I used to watch my mom shoplift and I used to pray and ask God to protect her and protect me. Sadly, my mother was arrested a few times for selling drugs and shoplifting. She eventually went to prison a few times during my younger life. My mom was a strong woman and she still took care of our needs when she was not around. She would assign somebody else to take care of us.

When I became a teenager, I started hanging out with my friends and we used to smoke and drink every day. I used to do stupid things at times with girls and it was just very crazy. I don't know how I graduated but I did in 1996. I was doing drugs, smoking weed, drinking and hanging out with my girlfriends. I was really good at basketball but I ruined it because I wanted to hang out and kick it with my boys and do stupid things.

My Mom Went to Prison

When I finished high school, my mother went to prison for five-and-half years. Then my grandmother died. I started stealing and doing stupid things just to survive because I didn't have my mother, father or grandmother around to help. One time, I went to the store and stole some Black and Mild cigars because I didn't have any money. A police guy yelled at me, "Come back! Stop!" But I didn't stop. I just kept running. However, as I continued to run, something inside me told me to turn myself in. So I turned around and sincerely confessed, "I'm sorry." They took me to jail at the age of eighteen, and thank God I had someone to bail me out six hours later. Thank God for my Aunt Cynthia Bruner.

I went to court a month later and the judge sentenced me to twenty days in the county jail. At that time, I was very scared and nervous. Little did I know that God had a plan for me. I hate to proclaim it but that's where I met God, in my jail cell. I knew of God but I'd never met God. He used my cellmate to read the Bible to me and that's when God started showing me revelations about himself.

Fortunately, God showed me a vision that he wanted me to move to California because He had a plan for me. When I got out of jail, to my great surprise, my brothers asked me to move to San Diego, California with them! I couldn't believe it, but I knew that this was not a coincidence but God's plan. I said, "Thank you Jesus!"

So I moved to San Diego in December 1999. I didn't know what was going to happen. I started doing a job at Polinsky Children's Center when I was nineteen years old. At first, I thought the job was not for me, but soon I realized that the children really needed me. Working at Polinsky Children's Center improved my attitude, and taught me patience, kindness, and love. It also taught me how to be sharing and caring toward people. I did not know that God was shaping me to be the man I am right now through this job. For example, kids spit, kick, punch, bite, and curse at staff. It takes a great deal of compassion and patience to serve them each day. And this is what God has done in my life through them. God helped me realize that this job was going to help me to become an asset to the community. I have been promoted several times and now I am currently a Residential Care Worker Supervisor for the county of San Diego.

I started going to church across the street from where I used lived. It was a small church. One day I was heading to work and this person named Kim Lewis was riding a bike. He came up to me, while I was getting into my car and asked me if I like would like to do a Bible study. I responded, "Sure, why not." The following day I went to his house to do personal Bible study with him. He taught me about how to live as a Christian—meaning, how to depend on God, get to know God more, and how to yield to his Holy Spirit to live Christ's power through me such as in tithing and sharing my faith. Through time I also learned how and why it is important to consistently attend church services regularly with other followers of Christ as well as how to help and minister to people. I learned so much! However, the most important matter I learned was that the God (Jesus Christ) died on a cross for ALL of my sins, he was buried, and on the third day he physically resurrected from the grave. I was greatly touched to learn that God wanted to be my personal Lord and Savior and let me walk in life with him each day. I pondered about all of these things, and I still am so happy to say that on April 4, 2000 I made the decision to accept Christ Jesus. I felt like God gave me a new life.

My First Time in the Ocean

When I was nineteen, I got baptized at La Jolla Cove at midnight. It was pretty scary because that was the first time I had ever been in the ocean. I served Christ for three and a half years; but remorsefully I then turned my back on the Lord. At this time, I knew one day that I would return to him. He was so patient with me and allowed me to do my own thing for a short time. I thank him for his faithfulness and patience. I finally returned back to Christ in 2004. I started going to New Harvest Church with my co-worker Jesús Sandoval who had recently became a pastor.

I was even more dedicated and I started leading Bible studies at my house. I started doing personal Bible studies. I started preaching God's word. I then started leading Bible study classes at my church. I started picking up people in the van for church. I became the head usher. I just started doing a whole lot of things for the Lord. I stopped drinking, I stopped smoking, I stopped having sex with different types of women and I stopped doing all that type of junk that had kept me back.

God has completely changed me from the inside to the outside. I have been serving him for a total of seventeen years now. God eventually gave me a beautiful wife, Monique Bruner, and we now have two beautiful children, Dominique and Donnell Bruner Jr.

Before I married my wife, we did things the right way. We did not hug or kiss for like a year and a half. God blessed our wedding. It was very unbelievable. Now I'm serving God, loving people, and being who God called me to be.

Amen.

Chapter 5
Anointed From Birth

Justin Floyd

◆━━◇━━◆━━◇━━◆

"Now it is God who makes both us and you stand firm in Christ. He anointed us, set his seal of ownership on us, and put his Spirit in our hearts as a deposit, guaranteeing what is to come."

—2 Corinthians 1:21-22

My name is Justin Floyd. I am now forty years old. Once upon a time, I never believed I would make it to twenty-five. Me and my brother Jacob were born in San Diego. My early years were a blur. My father, Johnny, was a functional alcoholic. He finally got cleaned up, however, not too long after he passed away. We were left fatherless and there was a void I didn't know how to fill.

CHAPTER 5

When my father passed away, my mother sunk into drug addiction and with that came abusive relationships. Me and my brother were witnesses to all of it. I tried to be a father to my brother the best I could, but as a child trying to teach another child ended up just being a recipe for disaster. I created a monster trying to make him strong.

We went through many thins. We had a lot of pain, and we didn't know how to deal with it. We started smoking marijuana early and drinking alcohol. I was always ambitious, but raised on social security we were poor. I saw most of the young people around me with cars and other nice things in life. I began to want more. So I started selling drugs and followed what I learned from the streets. My mother, who was a functional addict, worked by day and sold drugs by night to make ends meet. I always loved and honored my mother no matter what she was. She was all I had left besides my brother.

My brother and I started gang banging looking for a father maybe, looking to fill the void in our lives. I was shot one day in an alley in the face and in the back at the age of sixteen years old. Miraculously the bullets missed every vital organ, my spine, everything.

That did not deter me but instead it made me and my brother angry and fueled the fire in us. Not long afterwards, I was shot in the head on University Avenue. My brother witnessed it and was traumatized more. I remember falling and my brother holding me. I was conscious and asked him if it skinned me. I thought I would be dead if it penetrated my brain like in the movies. My brother told me it just skinned me. Despite the odds, I survived again. This time the bullet shattered my skull and I had to have brain surgery and recover from a coma.

My brother was angrier than ever. He then was convicted after a shooting at age seventeen and given a sentence of twenty-five years to life. I sunk into drug addiction and was sent to prison with my brother. We were in the same cell. Then we went our separate ways. I got out and continued to mask my life's pain with more drugs and alcohol. When I got off parole, I found myself back in prison soon afterward. I was lost, with no direction in life. It was a revolving door with no exit. This went on into my mid-thirties. I was lost and finally getting tired. But I didn't know how to change the only life I had ever known.

Eventually, I reconnected with some old friends. I began to start going to church and it was there that I found my purpose in life—Jesus Christ my Lord and Savior. My life changed. God gave me a beautiful wife, children, a job and much more. I was given salvation, freedom and purpose. Jesus filled the void. Then I realized God had covered and prepared me and anointed me from birth for this.

Reader Reflections

Did you grow up in a single parent home? If so how has that effected you?

_____

_____

_____

_____

_____

_____

_____

_____

_____

_____

Did your parent(s) have any kind of addictions that you witnessed?

_____

_____

_____

_____

_____

_____

_____

_____

_____

_____

_____

Have you or a loved one experienced any form of violent injury?

_____

_____

_____

_____

_____

_____

_____

_____

_____

_____

_____

Chapter 6
Morals And Values

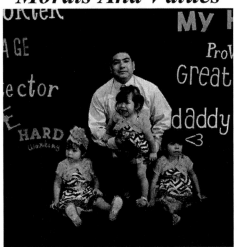

Joaquin Mena

<hr />

In my earliest memories, I recall walking to the store with my mom and sister and seeing drug addicts in the street. I don't know how I knew that they were homeless and did all that they did to support their drinking and drugging. I remember them collecting cans and asking for money, then getting angry and hostile when they were turned down with a food offering. I used to walk away and wonder to myself, "Why do they do that to themselves?" It didn't make any sense. I thought, "This isn't going to be life for me."

One thing I did understand was one of my father's biggest qualities. It was to defend himself, his family and his friends. I remember taking on the responsibility of protecting my sister when my father was not around. In particular, there was a boy who was in my sister's class who used to bully and pick on her until one day I ran towards him with full force. Due to the distance between us, he got a chance to climb a fence, and at that time I didn't know how to climb fences being younger. I was in preschool. However, I was able to attack the fence as he climbed up. Another time, I bit a dog who bit my sister.

It was a noble feeling, being able to defend my sister. I knew I had to put fear and other feelings aside for the greater good. Later, I found out that my dad and uncles were in a gang and understood it as a bigger defense system. Little did I know it was all smoke and mirrors. My dad went to prison for an array of criminal activities that included narcotics, an arsenal and a bunch of stolen goods. I didn't really know at the time why people would just bring him stuff until later, when I put the pieces together they were trading them for drugs. Not only did my dad deal drugs but he also did them, although, this is something I didn't know back then either. I did know he beat my mother so bad that he sent her to the hospital with a broken cheek bone. This is when I knew I wouldn't ever hit girls.

It's Generational

That's when my mother decided to leave and take me and my sister to my grandmother's house. There we got to hang out with all my mom's family, where almost every single male traditionally joined a gang in the neighborhood where we all lived in East San Diego. We have about five generations invested in the gang life. By generations, we mean age groups, as each generation only lasts about 10 years before the next group of little vatos rise up and form a new clique. My family has a couple members in almost every clique. We are a big family. We're actually one of the biggest families in the hood, not including all the ones that didn't join. We used to have birthday parties at least once a month and all the homies were invited. I still love the smell of carne asada on the grill and chicken al carbon. I remember as a kid running past my uncles to go get a piece of carne straight off the grill but I used to get caught by someone who needed a gofer to go for a beer and another one for their friend. Everyone knew the kids were perfect gofers and nobody questioned them going in the cooler. I remember sneaking beers up the tree. It would be like four of us sharing a beer up there. I can still hear the old school bumpin out somebody's lowrider while people stand around with their arm around their ladies. At that age, I knew what I wanted and it was simple—a lowrider and a firme hyna. If we could minus the drive-bys I wouldn't mind, but either way I knew the drill, just hit the floor and try to get behind something.

One summer night, I was already inside watching "The Simpsons" on TV when I heard shooting. I didn't really care too much since it wasn't at our house this time. About thirty minutes later I noticed the police and ambulances outside as people gathered. This time I was told to stay inside. I didn't realize what happened until the next day when I went outside and everything was gone. They didn't even bother to clean up the blood. There was a small crucifix laying on top of it. I knew someone had died there.

There were more shootings that summer and closer together. It was getting crazy and now even my cousin had a gun. I knew it was for our protection and it made me feel safe. I knew I was getting older and would soon be of age to join the gang, but either way I already felt we needed to stay together and protect each other. I started to play fight more, mimic attacks and prepare myself for what was to come. At age thirteen, I joined the gang and started meeting all the other kids my age who were joining or going to join, even the girls. We use to ditch and go drink and smoke weed, walk around and hit people up, and write on the walls until it started getting dark. Then everyone use to go to a spot called la posta, but I used to break off into my own little sub group if I could. Otherwise, I'd risk running into one of my older family members there and they would send me home. It was kind of embarrassing. Now that I think back I can see that maybe that did protect me, since a couple of kids in my age group who went to school with me ended up getting juvenile life and are still locked up today.

As more and more of my friends were getting locked up, I started to focus more on getting my firme Hyna and I've got to say I was successful. Before I was old enough to drive, my firme Hyna got pregnant, and there I was a fifteen-year-old kid with a kid. I dropped out of school and started to work full-time. I partied on the weekends. Occasionally, the homies would need me during the week, so I'd leave my fifteen-year-old baby momma at home with the baby on her own. She had my mom there to help, but now I know it's not the same. I had a duty to fulfill though. Whenever the homies called, I jumped with honor. I couldn't disgrace myself, right?

Well I ended up losing my baby momma and my kid to my duty. This only led to more partying and more alcohol and more weed and even meth. Summing up, it was depression and a whole lot of blur mixed with insanity. I started doing things I thought I would never do, like hitting my girlfriend. I was hanging around people I wasn't comfortable with. I was putting myself in dangerous situations and worst of all, the meth. Pretty soon, I was homeless and crazy and hostile like the people I've seen before. I was heart-broken because of what I had become. I was dusted and disgusted. I was seeing shadow people. There was someone watching me all the time; someone was out to get me, and everybody I had was in on it. My mom sent me to a crazy home where someone saw the same shadow figure that appeared right in front of me. What was going on!?!?

Reader Reflections

Do you let fear cloud your judgment?

_____

_____

_____

_____

Are you ashamed of things that are good for you?

_____

_____

_____

Do you do things that go against your morals and values?

_____

_____

_____

_____

_____

_____

Have you had undeniable coincidences that seem like a supernatural influence on your life?

_____

_____

_____

_____

_____

MORALS AND VALUES

What are some of your morals and values?

_____

_____

_____

_____

_____

What were your childhood dreams?

_____

_____

_____

_____

_____

_____

_____

_____

_____

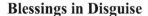

Blessings in Disguise

Finally, I got locked up for a good amount of time. While I was fighting a case, two of my uncles got killed and I was in there unable to do anything. Then I got out on G.S.U. and start getting back to "normal;" but after testing dirty a few times they sent me to a program where I sobered up and got on the scared straight program. I had two strikes and knew if I got locked up again that I might never get out. So I jumped through every hoop the probation put in front of me until I got off.

I continued to use the tools I learned in the program and it helped me to stay clean for two years. I matured a lot during that time. I started to make amends with my family. I was going to N.A. meetings but it was just a religion, going to the same meetings all the time. I was getting spiritual being of service but still wasn't letting God in my life. Then I lost the best job I ever had, and sadly had a lot of down time. I got depressed and began to drink again, and I got into a relationship as a spur of the moment thing. Next thing I knew, I had a set of twins that I so much petitioned to abort and another kid on the way, with my addiction still progressing. Then, finally I was back on meth.

Reader Reflection

Do you have any failed attempts that you can use for a future success?

_____

_____

_____

Have you let minor setbacks turn into major setbacks?

_____

_____

_____

_____

_____

Do you slide into situations or do you decide to be in a situation?

_____

_____

Me and my pregnant girlfriend were fighting all the time. Little did I know she was on meth too. Somewhere in between all of this, one of my best friends was killed, one of my uncles died from an infection due to IV drug use, and my grandpa died of pneumonia. Then my baby was born positive for meth. When this happened, Child Protective Services was on our backs. Thank God, I had already gotten clean before. I could jump all the same hoops again and be rid of C.P.S, but only this time I knew I had to up my program to something more to help me stay clean.

With all this drama, I just wanted to be a normal person. I was tired of losing people and going back to the same thing over and over again—jails, institutions, and death. I didn't know what it was going to take. I knew I had to let go of my baby momma cause she couldn't stay clean and even stopped trying. So, I was alone with a three-month-old and two one-year-olds but I was turning all the pain and all the fear of failing into hope, into hope that somehow I could get to live a normal life.

So I began to go to meetings again and I had a sponsor. Instead of doing a service commitment in the rooms of N.A., I was doing them in the community, where there are other recovering gang members and addicts getting out of themselves and giving back to the hood in a positive way—reaching and teaching the youngsters a better way of living. It's called Youth Empowerment. I was volunteering for a diversion program called Community Wraparound for gang-involved youth, but there was still something missing that I didn't even realize until I stepped foot into the church for the first time. Then it all set into place this indescribable feeling of peace and love and comfort. Suddenly, I realized there really was someone watching me all those years. It was God! And yes, there are things that can make my life miserable again but only if I let them! I've had plenty of reasons to give up but I didn't use them cause at the end of the day it would just have been another excuse.

I got saved—I surrendered my life to Jesus Christ. I then got baptized, and got involved in ministry. I go to church two days a week plus I still volunteer at the diversion program. But oh, doing all this is not just a religion, it's something way more! It's accepting and letting God in and developing a relationship with the Master of all that there is, was, and ever will be! It's letting go of all the shame and guilt and all the fear and doubt. Now I get to be a good example for my four beautiful daughters. I get to raise my kids and show them something beautiful instead of all the pain.

Reader Reflections

Do you use plausible but untrue excuses to give up?

_____

_____

_____

_____

Do you have pain or fear that you can turn into hope?

_____

_____

_____

_____

_____

_____

_____

_____

Do you trust God with all your worries and cares?

_____

_____

_____

_____

_____

_____

_____

Chapter 7
I Found My Treasure

Lucia Sandoval

<hr />

As I take myself back to my childhood, I remember being away from my parents for months at a time. During that period of my life, I didn't understand why I had to live with my relatives. I remember feeling lonely and thinking that I might never see my parents again.

My parents migrated from Mexico to work in the fields of Florida, while my big brother Gabe and I stayed behind in San Diego. They would come down to visit us like every six months for about two weeks. But they had to leave without saying goodbye because we would start crying.

The first time they left for Florida, they left my youngest

brother, Jesús, with my aunt. He was six months at that time and they were gone for a couple of months. Once they got settled in a camp, they came back to pick up my brother. To my mom's surprise, my brother didn't want to go with her, he wanted to stay with my aunt. I'm assuming that he thought my aunt was his mom. My mom was so broken hearted that she kept him with her until he got comfortable. Then they went back to Florida.

I also remember that as I went to the 1st grade at Central Elementary School, I would think to myself and pretend that my mom was in my school watching over me. I think that kept me from getting sad.

Three years later, I heard the best news ever! My parents had sent two tickets for me and my brother to fly to Florida. During that time, I had just finished 3rd grade and my brother had finished 5th grade.

Even though we lived in a camp in Florida, I remember those were some of the best times of my life. We didn't have much, but my family was together! The camp where we lived was huge with many workers. During the couple of years that my parents were there, they had worked their way up. They were pretty much running the camp, but with that, came a lot of hard work and responsibilities.

As I was meeting other kids in my school, I realized that we didn't have a nice house or nice clothes. That made me feel ashamed and embarrassed. I didn't want my friends to know where I lived. I think that is when I started to feel insecure about myself.

Back to California

Almost two years later, we all moved back to San Diego. This time we came back with another addition to our family! My baby brother Luis had been born in Florida. We came back when he was six months old. A couple of months later another brother was born, Manuel. He was only ten months younger than Luis! I remember my friend' s mom asking me if my parents had a television. I think that's what people would say when there were many kids in a family. Kind of funny now that I think about it. But that's how we stayed, a family of seven: mom, dad, my four brothers and me.

I have to say, I really didn't enjoy being the second oldest and the only girl. I had to help my mom with my two youngest brothers and all the chores around the house. I would usually help her with Luis. My parents were pretty strict with me. They would let me go to my friend's house, who lived around the corner for only forty-five minutes. Sometimes I would have to take my little bother with me.

As we got older and we were all in school, it got a little easier for me. But my parents were still strict with me. Sometimes I chose to lie in order to get what I wanted. I remember ditching school with my friend and going across the border to Tijuana. The next day, I would write a note to excuse myself for not being in school, with my mom's signature. Of course, she had no clue; amazingly, I never got caught. This encouraged me to do it a couple more times.

In high school, I started doing better in my last two years. I guess I was getting more focused in wanting to graduate. During this time, I had already gotten drunk a few times, mostly at parties or with friends. It was pretty much normal for my family to drink.

Tijuana Clubbing

After I graduated high school, I got a little wild. I left my house and moved in with my oldest brother, who already had two kids of his own. At that time I had a part-time job at a convalescent center, doing laundry. I wasn't satisfied with my job, but it provided me with money to party on the weekends. At first, my brother was not too happy to see me go out. At times, I would stay out all night. But I had already told him that if he got on my case, then I would move out. That is when I really did anything I wanted! I was going to the clubs in TJ (Tijuana) and getting drunk every weekend. I was always meeting guys but I didn't want to get serious with anybody. In my mind, all guys were players. So I was going to play them before I got played. That was my mentality back then.

Before I knew it, I was back at my parents' house. I started going to cosmetology school. I guess I can say, that's what I always wanted to do. Being back at my parents didn't change my party life. My parents didn't get on my case because they didn't want me to leave again.

My brothers would call me a drunk and a hoochie. Even though I pretended as if their words did not bother me, they were hurting me. At times, I would be by myself in my room and start crying. I felt lonely and lost. Deep inside, I knew my brothers were right. But I wasn't ready to change. I kept my wild life for a few more years.

I will always remember how my life finally changed. My younger brother, Jesús, had started going to a New Harvest church. He had approached me a few times and invited me to go to church, but I never went. One time he came over when I was about to leave to a club. He said, "Lucia, if you don't repent, you're going to go to hell!" My response was, "It's ok. I'll party in hell." I still remember this, because my brother brings it out, every now and then, in his preaching. He's now a pastor.

The moment that changed my life was at my brother's wedding. That was my first time going to a Christian church. The ceremony was so beautiful that I said to myself, "That's what I want when I get married!" Soon after that, I gave my life to the Lord Jesus Christ and never looked back.

The Altar

I remember going to the altar and telling God, "God if you're real, then remove my desire to drink alcohol and replace it with something else." People that knew me back then knew that I didn't have a sweet tooth. Well, I guess I can say that the Lord took away my desire for alcohol and replaced it with my sweet tooth. Now I've been sober for over 20 years. And if you know me now, you know that I love pastries!

At this present time, I'm so happy serving the Lord. I'm no longer empty, lonely, or hurt. It's been a process but Christ has truly changed me. I've traveled to other countries. I've seen how God has moved in other people's lives. I couldn't see myself doing anything else or living without God in my life!

I thank God for watching over me and my family while we were still living our lives without any cares in the world. I could have been killed, but the Lord graciously had another plan for my life! Jesus Christ can also move in your life and in your situation. All you have to do is give your life to him and he will do the rest.

Chapter 8
The Reflection Of A Woman

Christina Torres

I stand in front of a broken mirror, the reflection of a woman who has gone through so much, she appears to be shattered, broken hearted and hurt. During our trials in life we come across people or situations that try to destroy our images, break down our spirit, victimize us and defeat us. I am not defeated. Today I stand bolder than ever. God draws near to the broken-hearted; he heals the open wounds of those who are shattered. He brings peace to those who are hurt. We just have to believe. Have faith versus fear, confidence versus compromises. We have to trust and lean on God's will and not on our own understandings. Through our problems in life, our Lord brings promises. Do not be a victim of this world but a victor in his kingdom. I, Christina, am a follower of Jesus Christ and I will rise from the ashes. Amen.

How many times have we stopped to think about the past? What things have we gone through that define our character today? How have our life experiences impacted us for better or worse? I will share with you how my higher power has changed my life.

As the first born, I felt like I was a mistake. My mom was only sixteen years old when she gave birth to me. How was she able to love or be prepared for a child at such a young age? I would question these things because I grew up feeling like I was not someone she desired but only an unexpected obligation. When my brother was born, I saw how she favored him. They shared a stronger bond. Regardless of the doubts I carried, I still admired the strong woman she was.

My mom was a single mother throughout the years because my father was in and out of jail. He was very controlling and verbally abusive toward us and it led up to my parents' separation. My father suffered a depression after my mom left and it gave him a reason to use drugs. My mom was unaware of his drug usage. I was aware. I witnessed his self-destructive behaviors. I loved my dad very much. I felt I could not leave him alone to suffer on his own. I stayed to take care of my dad at the age of thirteen. I was going through mixed emotions, feeling overwhelmed by the dysfunction in our home, the yelling, the fighting, the tears and the fears that were caused by drugs. I felt alone. I didn't have anyone to talk to. I was not allowed to have many friends because I was controlled by my father.

I felt unloved by my mother. I felt like I wanted to die. Instead I rebelled. I started to wander off on my own, thinking I could numb my feelings and fill the emptiness of my life by drinking alcohol. I developed vulnerability instead. I started hanging out with the wrong crowd and by the age of fifteen I was using methamphetamine, smoking marijuana and was involved in gang activities. I was living a destructive lifestyle. I dropped out of high school, was expelled for numerous fights and I was in the juvenile probation system until the age of eighteen. So many events and tragedies occurred, even throughout my adulthood, yet I knew in my heart that I did not want to live in corruption for the rest of my life.

I did not know God like I know him today, but I always felt his presence. I felt the Lord's grace over my life when I witnessed my friend who passed away in my arms from gunshot wounds. I felt the Lord's protection when I was being physically abused by a man who claimed he was driven by the devil to cause harm upon me. I felt the Lord's mercy when I was driving intoxicated and was involved in a car accident. I felt the healing hand of the Lord over my broken heart after the death of my first aunt and a dear boyfriend. I felt the Holy Spirit battling the spirits of drug addiction, alcoholism, depression and discouragement within me. I have seen the wonders and miracles he has done for not only me but for my father, who has recovered and been given salvation.

Today, I have a better relationship with my mother and I am also a blessed mother to an adorable child. God sent me a piece of heaven, my son. I am thankful and grateful because without God I would not be where I am today. I am loved and I am blessed.

Chapter 9
Here To Remain

Sienna Gomez

My name is Sienna Gomez. I will soon be nineteen. In my short years, I have not only lived but I have also died in between. I believe I have been through various struggles so that I can find my own hidden treasure and be a blessing to others.

Growing up, love was easy and it was around. I could feel it, see it and believe I was a part of it. But growing up with love also comes with a thin line of hate. I was raised by my mother. Seeing her as a single mother gave me an inner strength that I didn't quite know was there. But when life got harder, my strength came to me in ways I couldn't describe. It also wearied my heart. I was exposed to domestic violence in my home life, both physical and emotional, then also later because of who I decided to love.

That's where my hate came in. I craved the feeling of affection where I left my heart to rot. The best times in my life are also the times where my life was a blur. I struggled with reality, so I changed my own in ways a young woman shouldn't. It led me to alcohol, young and misguided love, relationships with people who were only there for temporary reasons. Although these times in my life were fun and exciting, they were also a nightmare that I couldn't wake up from.

Fast forwarding, I was also raped. When that man raped me, he took a part of me that was not only physical but mental. I was lost; I forgot who I was, and then I found the strength my mother taught me as a young girl. This time it was different. I was now a role model to my younger sisters and my cousins. Although I had no sense of direction, they gave it to me clearly. I was angry, bitter, and confused sometimes, and I still am. But I'm learning not to be mad. I do not hate that man who laid hands on me or the men who have abused me or my family. My sisters who are young and innocent taught me how to be just that again.

I have learned that those who have hurt you are just as hurt. Hurt people hurt people. So although the pain they have caused seems so unfair at the moment, we have to love and forgive the broken. Because we all have been broken or the breaker. In addition, I have met great people within my journey, from strangers on public transportation who came to sit with me while I was in tears, to mentors, counselors and teachers I have been ultimately blessed to encounter.

I guess I could say my hidden treasures are the people I meet on the way. My sisters Krimsynn, Cyann and Goldynn are three of the greatest that any girl could have. And the rest of my family, although this was where some of my deepest pains lie, has also been the strongest foundation of love. And that remains.

Reader Reflections

Have you felt love before? Explain:

_____

_____

_____

_____

_____

_____

_____

_____

_____

_____

_____

_____

_____

_____

_____

_____

_____

_____

Do you love yourself?

_____

_____

_____

_____

_____

_____

_____

_____

_____

_____

_____

Have you forgiven the people who have hurt you?

_____

_____

_____

_____

_____

_____

_____

_____

_____

_____

_____

_____

_____

Chapter 10
Strengthened By Their Strength

Dr. Ali Freedman, PsyD, MsBA

My hidden treasures are the people around me, with whom you'd think I have little in common. I'm Jewish psychologist who's fluent in the irreverent humor and language one learns growing up working in a mechanic's shop in New Jersey. While this description may lead you to believe many things about me and my preferences, one of my favorite places to be is Community Wraparound—surrounded by current and former gang members, the majority of whom are in various stages of Christianity including being Christian Faith leaders.

There was one week when I was in church four days in a row and I wondered if I'd tell my (legitimately Jewish) mother about that, given that I had not been in a synagogue that many times in twenty years. Community Wraparound is where I can commune with my no longer hidden treasures.

These youth and mentors have been through everything. Parents dying. Incarceration. Abuse and neglect of every kind. Domestic violence. Familial substance use and mental illness. Insufficient food. Homelessness. Literally in the last week we have discussed every single one of these items as current and relevant issues. After putting in my time in my day job—(over)working in social services—why on earth does putting in time until nine on Monday nights with this crew recharge my battery?

They say therapists become therapist to heal themselves. Is that why? Certainly, I've got healing to do but you would think the sixty or so hours I put in at my day job would take care of that. I know that helping people feeds my soul. But I believe it's the natural and mutual evolution in Community Wraparound that lights me up. I like to think that I have some things to offer from my professional and academic training, and I do. But outside of some really heart wrenching and scary events—active psychosis, responses immediately after a sexual assault, coping with tragic deaths including suicide and murder in the community, de-escalation of a youth with a weapon, and some modest fundraising—I'd say my professional skills have come in less handy than my heart and my willingness to follow rather than lead. And without a doubt, the amount that I have learned and received from this community has fed my spirit in ways I cannot begin to describe.

I smile there. I laugh there. I learn there. I love there.

Throughout this experience I have met so many teachers,

so many healers, and so many heroes. As a result, I have felt that what I had to share couldn't compare to what others have contributed. I didn't think I had anything as important to say as everybody else. But I'm so impressed by what I hear every week from the youth and mentors who are the real teachers, that I wanted to offer these brief words as a learner and as one who cherishes the gift to be able to join this group. I go to Wrap every week and regardless of what is going on with me, I smile there. I laugh there. I learn there. I love there.

It is in Community Wraparound that I have met some of the strongest people I've ever known.

There are many participants in Community Wraparound who motivate me, and I am in awe of one particular young woman who has lived through more in less than two decades than most people do in a lifetime. She aces the ACE (Adverse Childhood Experiences) questionnaire, if you know what I mean, but she has translated that adversity into an inner strength that inspires me. Everything that I learned in school as meeting the definition of a trauma, she takes it in like a vitamin—each challenge further fortifying her spirit and empowering her to navigate this crazy, unfair world with confidence and grace. She's stronger every day I see her. She's smarter every day I see her. She's more sensitive, compassionate, and inspiring...every day I see her.

I love a mother who shows up week-in and week-out with her family, even though her older son is often incarcerated all the while she battles homelessness—a homelessness that could be more easily addressed if she wasn't fervently committed to being available to her son on probation. It's harder to find a home when you have limited financial resources and your application comes with frequent searches by law enforcement because a member of the family is a probationer. Mom compromises every personal comfort so she can find a shelter for her son to give him the best chances to get on the right track, and then she secures shelter for herself and her other children. Then she and other mothers like this still volunteer to help make food for Community Wraparound. They make every court date for their kids. They still nurture their younger one's dreams—bringing a younger child to an Open House at the Police Station because of a goal to be a police officer, as just one example.

I celebrate the father who shares his violent past and drug use not like a badge and not to glorify it, but rather with reflection on how he now understands his behavior and he hopes others can learn from...and prevent the pain associated with his mistakes. He recognizes how much of his life he gave away in prison, often in solitary confinement. He dedicates every available moment he has to save youngsters from making those same mistakes. He hopes against all else that his time served can serve in place of the youth he mentors.

I honor another father who was released from prison and came to Community Wraparound apologizing to his adult son for not being there and telling him how proud he was of him. And he did this in a circle of thirty-five people he had never met. His son received that message with his Community Wraparound family around him. All the youth, mentors, and volunteers also heard what they needed to hear in that sharing. Father and son were not the only ones choking back tears. Many of us weren't bothering to cover them up.

What happens in Community Wraparound is sacred and it is private. While I can think of a specific person for each of the above scenarios, their privacy is guarded by the fact that I can name at least three people who fit each of the above stories just from our small community in recent weeks.

I used to joke that one of the best things about being involved in Community Wraparound is that I get to do good without having to do a bunch of documentation and billing. But the true joy is meeting people like these heroes who have overcome incredible adversity and who give so much of themselves when others may look at them and think how little they have to give. Judgment is a funny thing. Perspective is a funny thing. Who's giving and who's receiving is a really funny thing. More and more I realize that I go to Community Wraparound in large part for me. To be strengthened by their strength. To be humbled by their resolve. To be awed by their perseverance.

There are many things about my heroes in Community Wraparound I hope one day I can emulate when I grow up...someday. Sure, there are also things I hope the youth and mentors can grow out of. Maybe we can help each other. Maybe our whole community can help each other grow out of or grow into who we aim to be. Community is where our problems sometimes come from...but it is also where our answers lie.

A Quick Note

A quick note to young or even experienced mental health professionals.

Yes, professional boundaries are important and there are reasons for them. And yet, they are not as black and white as what you learn in your training. They are more permeable and flexible than that. To do truly valuable work, they have to be. My boundaries in my official work capacity would withstand scrutiny. But that's one of the other bonuses about being a volunteer in Community Wraparound—and having a few years and lessons behind me. I'm in a different place to be able to evaluate the ways in which I can help when I'm not fully cloaked in my professional role of a psychologist, which, ironically, is also strengthening the very professional rules and skills I temporarily check, when I walk through the Community Wraparound door. When in doubt, consult. You need your friends to help you stay on the path when it's more rocky, overgrown, and wild than it is in the textbooks.

Chapter 11
Resilience Blossoms

Dana Brown

My life forever changed on November 13, 2014 when I met Arthur and Gabby Soriano.

Police officer John Cooksey, from the Mid-City Division's Juvenile Services Team met this couple in the emergency room, where they had raced to join their son, Adrian. Jumped by some fellow peers at his high school, Adrian was bruised and bloody. Officer Cooksey went to the hospital to find out what had happened. He told the family about a youth leadership skill building opportunity, Youth Voice, hosted by the Mid-City Division weekly. He encouraged Arthur and Gabby to join him that afternoon. My memory of seeing the Soriano family walk through the door to Youth Voice is and will also be indelibly seared in my heart and soul.

Our poignant, powerful and profound collaborative relationship began!

I have been blessed and honored to spend many hours with Arthur and Gabby and their friends Robert and Gabriela Ontiveros, Juan Valderrama, and Pastor Jesús Sandoval (co-founders of Youth Empowerment). Our time vested together, gathered around the Sorianos dining room table, has been filled with hope and tears, sharing our hearts with each other.

As we've shared our heartbreaks, traumas, pains and angst, we have lifted each other up with hope and inspiration. We have continually inquired of each other, "How can we help others heal? How can we bring healing to our communities and neighborhoods? How can we ignite the systems (education, foster, juvenile justice, criminal justice, probation, law enforcement, etc.) in transforming their focus to helping not harming the ones they serve, to bring healing to others?"

As a social entrepreneur, ally and advocate for nineteen years, my passionate devotion in life is with transforming systems, cross-sector in a socio-ecological model, to integrate their policies, practices, procedures and programs with the understanding of the unified sciences of ACEs (Adverse Childhood Experiences). When we humans understand the impact of trauma (acute, chronic, vicarious, complex, systems-induced) on our brain neurologically and our body biologically, the impact of toxic stress, epigenetics and building resilience, we infuse the ACEs science and create systems reflective of cultures of care, hope and healing. It is the most critically imperative transformation needed in every system in our nation, including our own belief system.

As we, as a group, have explored the depth of community trauma and community violence on families' well-being, I've been profoundly blessed to mentor this team's innate leadership skills. Equally imperative, we have explored our capacities to heal and build individual and community resilience as we advocate for systems change.

Introducing Youth Empowerment's team to local leaders on community initiatives influencing policy change, our mutual intention has been transforming cross-sector systems to cultures of care and compassion. We are vested with policy change, specifically with the re-entry system. With recidivism hovering at 77% in our nation, noted in a Bureau of Justice Statistics study, we are raising awareness of the staggering costs of the criminal justice system in our country. Just as imperatively, we are educating inner city community members and families on their capacity to build resilience, heal and transform their families.

Arthur, Gabby and I, plus several others, participated in the three-day certificate training with Community Connections for Youth. The Bronx team engaged with several community members on February 25th and 26th back in 2015 with our Alternatives to Incarceration Training Institute.

I serve on the City of San Diego Commission on Gang Prevention & Intervention. In 2015, our Resolution Number R-

309894, supporting a trauma-informed approach to address and prevent gang violence was unanimously approved. Trauma informed care is an organizational structure and treatment framework that involves understanding, recognizing and responding to the effects of all types of trauma.

We commissioners and the Youth Voice leaders have inquired of each over, "How are we helping the families of active gang members? How are we providing services and wrapping around families in need of resources? How are we engaging families in becoming part of the solution in their neighborhoods and communities? How can we be part of the solution?"

The magnitude of the impacts on families of gang violence and community trauma is staggering. The hopelessness of not having access to care, the myriad disparities and social determinants of healthcare and the systems-induced trauma are horrific, unjust realities that affect every single member of the family across their life spans.

The cradle to prison pipeline must be transformed to the cradle to career pipeline. Myriad solutions are in place throughout our nation. Successful strategies being used locally and nationally include restorative justice, intersectional approaches, teen court, mock trials in criminal justice classes, young adult court and a trauma informed juvenile and criminal justice system.

Our criminal justice system is in dire need of providing healthy, safe neighborhoods and communities for formerly incarcerated individuals re-entering society. When these former inmates face adulthood without supportive family, housing, education, employment and other critical protective factors, their hopelessness is fed and their soul is starved.

A national study in 2014 by the Ella Baker Center for Human Rights reflects how the United States spends $80 billion every year to lock up more than 2.4 million people in jails and prisons. This far outpaces budgetary allocations and spending on housing, transportation, and higher education.

The solutions are within the communities. The healing is within the families. The hope lies within the individual.

Youth Empowerment is an example of groups devoted to supporting inner city youth and families. Others include Community Wraparound, National Conflict Resolution Center, Project AWARE, and Youth Voice. They are building resilience. Connecting hearts. Inspiring hope. Igniting change.

Arthur and Gabby Soriano, Ed and Aleyda Wales, Robert and Gabriela Ontiveros, Juan Valderrama, Pastor Jesús Sandoval, and Reginald Washington are human angels. How lucky am I to learn from and share with these amazing souls? How fortunate am I to be part of their families? How grateful am I to know all of them and their extended families? Very much so!

The California Endowment funded a professional filmmaker, Rita Grant, who brilliantly captured our collective work. The movie is called "Resilience Blossoms." You can view it on You Tube, so please watch it at https://www.youtube.com/watch?v=qoG-fZyWLYU.

An Invitation

Every Monday night at New Harvest Christian Fellowship in San Diego, community members from all faiths, backgrounds, and ages gather together in our cafeteria for meals. We spend time getting to know each other, share needs, and find support. Some moms bring homemade food. This is what we call a community wraparound. Some people have resources to help others, others do not but they share what they can.

Come feel loved and welcomed here, in this informal space, where we have our family photos on the wall.

This is what I'd hoped for all those years ago, when I entered my pastor Clem Casas' home for dinner for the first time and found the peace of God there. It was the pictures of family on his wall that made me feel that way. It was after dinner that he invited me to pray and connect with God. He fed me not only physically, leaving me with a full belly, but he also offered me spiritual food to fill my heart with something new.

You may feel alone but you can still have family and be part of a community.

Maybe you're someone who would like to help at-risk youth and you're looking for a way to get involved.

Maybe you want to get out of "the life" and have new life too.

Or maybe you'd simply like to share a meal with us, your neighbors.

Come if you'd like, no matter what your life has been like. We don't judge. Our stories show there is always hope. As Arthur Soriano has written in this book: "It *can* be done."

This is what Jesus Christ did, when he sat down and broke bread with friends of all kinds. Some criticized him for it but he replied, "It is not the healthy who need a doctor but the sick. I have not come to call the righteous, but sinners."

God loves *you* just the way you are, right where you are, completely. Come feel "at home" with us, among people who know both sides of life. We have "been there and done that." We have chosen to walk in the joy of redemption and we love to help others do the same.

Pastor Jesús Sandoval and Arthur Soriano,

New Harvest Christian Fellowship
3060 54th Street (in East San Diego)
San Diego, CA 92015
(619) 326-8450
www.newharvesteastsandiego.org
Arthur@youthempowermentsd.org

Community Wraparound

Back in the Day

Progression

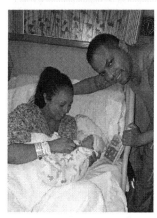

Today

Today

Please check out
www.BowmanPublishing.com
for more great books.